I AFFIRM MY POWER

Other Books by Phoebe Garnsworthy

Remember the Witch Within

Align with Soul

Lost Nowhere: A Journey of Self-Discovery (Vol. 1)

Lost Now Here: The Road to Healing (Vol. 2)

Daily Rituals: Positive Affirmations to Attract Love, Happiness, and Peace

The Spirit Guides: A Short Novella

Define Me Divine Me: A Poetic Display of Affection

and still, the Lotus Flower Blooms

Sacred Space Rituals

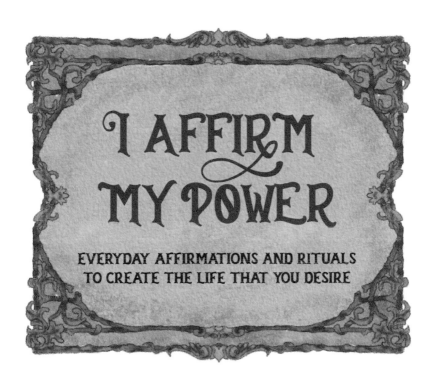

I AFFIRM MY POWER

EVERYDAY AFFIRMATIONS AND RITUALS
TO CREATE THE LIFE THAT YOU DESIRE

PHOEBE GARNSWORTHY

Andrews McMeel
PUBLISHING®

Andrews McMeel Publishing
a division of Andrews McMeel Universal
1130 Walnut Street, Kansas City, Missouri 64106

www.andrewsmcmeel.com
www.PhoebeGarnsworthy.com

23 24 25 26 27 SDB 10 9 8 7 6 5 4 3 2 1

ISBN: 978-1-5248-7933-4

Library of Congress Control Number: 2022945345

Editor: Katie Gould
Art Director: Holly Swayne
Production Editor: Dave Shaw
Production Manager: Tamara Haus
Illustrator: Jakub Szczepaniak

The contents of this book are the personal opinions of the author and intended for educational purposes only. This information does not substitute for any professional medical advice. Phoebe Garnsworthy does not accept any legal responsibility for any personal injury or damage arising from using the information in this book. If you decide to make a decision in regard to any form of your health, diet, or exercise, consult a health expert first.

Attention: Schools and Businesses

Andrews McMeel books are available at quantity discounts with bulk purchase for educational, business, or sales promotional use. For information, please e-mail the Andrews McMeel Publishing Special Sales Department: sales@amuniversal.com.

Take a deep breath and feel the love overflowing within you.
Take a deep breath and feel the energy of the Universe holding you.
And take one more deep breath and tell yourself—
everything is going to be all right.

Contents

From the Author

Hello, beautiful light warrior,

I see you. I know that you are trying hard every day to do your best and live the life that you desire, but you feel as though you are failing. You are seeking strength to persevere and guidance on how to step forward. I understand how you feel because I've been there. I've tried and I've failed. I've prayed and I've lost hope. I've found myself lost in a deep, dark place, confused as to how to ever get out. But I did get out. Because I believed that I could, and I want to show you how, too.

I wrote this book at a time of despair in my life. At a time when I felt out of alignment with my soul, when I was floating amidst the madness of uncertainty. I was struggling to find my anchor of breath, to feel grounded in my skin and secure in my space here on Earth. And most importantly, I had great trouble surrendering and trusting wholeheartedly into the magical workings of the Universe. But all of those struggles were in my head. Because I knew the truth of how to realign with the power of my divinity—I needed to get back into a healthy and spiritual routine. All that was required was a commitment to honor myself and my experience.

And so, I created this affirmation and manifestation book to share with you my routine. This perfect combination of daily rituals, spiritual practices, journaling, and meditation is what was needed to connect with my soul and feel the power of my truth once more. And within a short time of consistent repetition, I recognized myself again. I felt the echoing voice of my soul beating loudly in my heart, speaking love notes through my mind, and telling me that all is as it should be.

In these pages I will guide you through the simple techniques that I used to bring love and happiness back into my life. I will help guide you to reveal the divine light within you and to build the confidence within yourself and the trust in the Universe that you have been craving. All it takes is a commitment to yourself, to practice self-love and self-care on a daily basis.

Together we will create your sacred space to honor your soul. Your angels are here waiting to speak to you. The whole Universe is sending you love as it cheers for you. And we are all ready to watch you blossom into the person you have always dreamed of becoming. Transformation is here and ready for you if you want it.

I live with harmonious peace in my heart now, and I do not waiver from this truth. I walk with confidence in my skin, with a great sense of faith in the divine power of the Universe. But most importantly, I trust myself. I honor my soul, and I listen to the wisdom of my intuition. And the more I practice using all of these spiritual tools of self-love and self-care, the more me I feel, the freer I live, and the more blessed I look at each day.

Love, Phoebe

Deep Breaths

I feel such a heaviness in my body when I wake up.
My soul is yearning to move spaces, to switch places with another.
I lie in bed waiting for the sky to become light once more,
but the darkness is staying, and I need to get up.
I turn the music on, allowing the vibrations to awaken my energy,
and slowly, very slowly, I begin stretching my body.
The freedom of kicking my legs and moving my arms is liberating.
And I am reminded of the importance to give back to my body.
My breath supports the release of my pain.
And with every inhale and exhale, my skin is shedding.
I feel like my soul has been journeying to faraway lands through my dreams.
And even though I am awake, she doesn't want to come home yet.
Through my meditation I call her name.
She is listening but is still so far away.

I imagine the energy chakras of my body as I close my eyes and breathe deeply.

Inhale . . . The energy is swirling from my root chakra, tapping into the ancient
     wisdom from my ancestors.
Exhale . . . I release anything that does not serve me.

Inhale . . . I can see the energy circulating around my solar plexus, igniting
     confidence and power.
Exhale . . . I remove any limiting beliefs or fears from my mind.

Inhale . . . The energy is swirling my sacral chakra now, inviting creativity and
     immense pleasure.
Exhale . . . I let go of anything that does not serve me.

Inhale . . . My heart chakra is opening; the energy is moving around fluidly and vibrantly. I feel the love from the Universe enter my body and kiss me.

Exhale . . . I release any energy that is stagnant and holding me back from fulfilling my life purpose.

Inhale . . . My breath is cleansing my throat chakra now. I feel empowered to speak my truth and communicate with ease.

Exhale . . . I let go of any thoughts that are detrimental to my well-being.

Inhale . . . My third-eye chakra is opening as I breathe in the light energy around me. It's vibrating and clearing the pathway of my intuition.

Exhale . . . I release any impurities that are standing in my way, anything that is restricting my connection to my intuition.

Inhale . . . I feel the energy move from the base of my spine up to my crown chakra. Here the energy is released. I meet with the starry frost of Universal love. And here, I melt into my body a little bit more. For my soul is dancing above my head, above my body and my heart. I have liberated myself through my internal channel of light.

Exhale . . . The last of my skin has been shed; my soul is rejuvenated, nurtured and nourished. I feel completely at ease, at peace, and in the harmonic flow of the Universe.

And as I take my last breath, I feel a click above my head. Everything is now completely aligned. I stay in this moment of bliss for several minutes, allowing the energy to flow from the heavens high above. I feel a surplus of divine light energy move through the cosmos, into the skies above, and right through to the crown of my head. It moves down the center of my chakra line, and through my body, as it kisses the Earth. Here, the Earth anchors my presence as I hold this energy and allow myself to be the transmuter. Together, we are reenergized and empowered. I have connected to the divine source of creation.

In this space, I am free. In this space, I affirm my power.

Introduction

You are an alchemist of energy. Therefore, you can create any life that you desire.

You are divinely guided and supported along your life path, always, but sometimes you are challenged in ways that seem impossible to move forward. Sometimes we aren't challenged by other situations but by our own limitations of what we think we can achieve in this life. This book is a reminder to let you know that anything you want is possible. And it's not only possible; it's coming to you. Because you want it, because you crave it. Together, as we go through this book, you will learn how to fuel the fire within your existence to harness the goals you seek. Together, as we explore the limitless gifts of the Universe, you will discover the great power that you hold within, and you will feel the confidence needed to step into this power. In order to do this, you need to comprehend the fundamental truth of spiritual philosophy, which is "everything is energy."

Everything in the entire Universe is made of vibrating energy. That energy vibrates at a particular frequency. All of the manifestations that you crave are simply vibrating at a different frequency from what you are currently holding in your life. Like matter attracts like matter, and you have the power to call your chosen manifestation in, by choosing to emit the desired vibrational frequency first. Energy is never created or destroyed; it is merely transformed. Therefore, you need to learn how to be an alchemist of energy and transform your own energetic vibration into the frequency that you desire. And you have the power to do this very easily by implementing affirmations and daily rituals filled with spiritual practices and philosophies, such as the ones that I will share with you in this book. But the key to creating the life you desire relies heavily on your willingness to partake in these spiritual activities consistently. It doesn't just take one time to connect with your soul; you need to strengthen that bond and trust in that connection daily.

This book will teach you how to harness the Universal energies around you of Earth, Air, Water, Fire, and Spirit to assist you in your journey of transformation.

I will show you how to use these spiritual techniques to assist you on your path of personal development and great transformation. Everything that you crave is merely at your fingertips. The life that you desire will come to you when you listen to the words of your soul and have ultimate trust and faith in the workings of the Universe.

To use this book: Close your eyes and ask what you need to hear today. Open the book up at random and read the affirmation loudly. This affirmation will be your intention for your ritual. Ignite your ritual to honor your soul (explained in detail in the chapter "Creating Your Sacred Space"). Read the affirmation definition, and follow through by answering the journaling questions and meditation guidance (this will be your action that supports the calling in of your chosen manifestation). I will explain the powers of these spiritual practices in the following pages and how they will support your personal development growth.

All you need to change your vibrational frequency is dedication, participation, and determination. Let's explore your own energy first so that we may begin.

Listening to Our Energy

In order to transform your energy, we need to be aware of the energy you currently hold. Your energy changes all the time—every second, every day, in every activity that you do. Your energy is influenced by the words you say, the thoughts you think, and the events in your life that you consciously and unconsciously choose. Every area of your life is affecting your energy, for the good or bad. This is why it is crucial to be aware of your energy so that you can cleanse, recharge, and protect it often. When our energy is illuminated and grounded, we can continue living our best life in alignment with our soul.

Before commencing your energy work, first feel the energy within and around you by using the following technique:

Close your eyes and bring your awareness to your energy field. Ask yourself some questions to define the energy, such as:

What does my energy feel like?

What does my energy look like?

What color is it?

What texture is it?

Where exactly is it located?

How is the energy moving around me?

Is it sluggish or rapid?

Use descriptive words, such as sticky, dark, heavy, light, cloudy, or vibrant.

Once you have identified how your energy is, use your breath, visualization, and spiritual practices to transform that energy. The aim is for you to transmute your energy to flow fluidly with ease around your body, harmoniously without interference.

If your energy feels stuck, heavy, and cluttered, use your breath to channel that energy out of your body. Take long exhalations, forcing energy to be released quickly, and reciprocate with deep inhalations, welcoming new vibrations into its place. If your energy feels chaotic and spread out, use Earth energy to anchor your presence. Mother Nature can cleanse and recharge your energy through her potent power of nurturing love. She has the ability to transform any energy into lightness of being. If you have time, go for a walk in nature, connect with the soil under your feet. Or simply imagine a safe space surrounded in nature where you can allow your body to rest and regain its strength. Feel the weight of your body upon the Earth and allow it to support you. And lastly, if you feel your energy is unable to be found, trust that it is there and use water to cleanse yourself. Do this either metaphorically or physically, and imagine the Water energy washing away any impurities or darkness that is concealing your light. There are always solutions for whatever you are feeling. Your soul knows the truth; let it speak to you. And allow the beautiful energies of the Universe around you to soothe your energy.

To protect your energy, Fire energy holds great strength and resilience. Light a candle or imagine a ring of fire around you as you command your protection. Spend time defining that protective circle around your aura and ask your angels or spirit guides for assistance if needed. Imagine any negative energy melting into the fire. Trust that you are protected with love as you carry on throughout your day.

Practice tuning into your energy daily, before your ritual or whenever you feel like your soul needs change. When we are stuck in unhealthy life patterns, our energy will stop flowing, causing us resistance and pain. Or sometimes, our energy is moving too rapidly. As we live in a place of flight or fight, it's unable to be controlled, and we feel as if we are moving fast, with little or no control over our lives. Either way, your energy should be moving around you and within you at a steady, peaceful pace. And you have the power to create this space within; all you need to do is be aware and find the best spiritual tools that work for you. The more you implement these spiritual tools into your life—the more you practice cleansing, aligning, and recharging your energy—the easier it will be to attune your vibration to attract the manifestations that you desire.

Affirmations and Manifestations

Affirmations are sound energy. They are powerful spiritual tools that carry specific vibrational frequencies that can assist you in creating the life that you desire. Every word that you speak is a conversation with the Universe, and this conversation has the ability to cocreate your destiny. The question is: What is it that you crave in your life, and what frequency is the energy that you wish to embody today? Of that desired energy, how often do you speak words that support it? How often do you act in alignment with it? Are you choosing to surround yourself with people, situations, and activities that embody the energy you wish to acquire?

Speaking an affirmation of what you desire is the first step toward embodying it. Consciously making choices that support your desired affirmation will be the key factor in achieving your manifestation.

An affirmation is an assertive statement that confirms what you wish already exists—such as, "I am powerful." You may not feel powerful, but saying that you are changes your energy vibration. There are scientific studies that prove your brain reacts in the exact same way whether you visualize partaking in an activity or physically do it. So when we state an affirmation and imagine ourselves doing something that shows the affirmation is true, we are literally changing our own energetic vibration within our body and mind. And when we change our energetic vibration, we can, in turn, attract those same vibrations in. Like matter attracts like matter. The more we choose to vibrate at our desired frequencies, the easier it will be to live the life that we are craving.

But speaking our affirmations and saying our manifestations out loud is only the beginning. We need to ensure that our actions and choices in life support our wishes. Imagine that you are seeking peace. You are saying peaceful affirmations in the morning, but then during the day you find yourself yelling at street traffic, spending time with friends who gossip negatively, or refusing to take time out of your day to walk in nature and harmonize your energy flow.

Even though we can desire one thing, we can consciously be acting against it. So be sure to check in with yourself, be self-aware with your actions, and choose your thoughts wisely.

Let's imagine an ideal scenario. You are seeking peace. You say, "I am peaceful." And with each action you ensure that you are cleansing your mind of unimportant thoughts through spiritual practices. You prioritize your health by eating foods that bring you nutrition and healing. You spend time doing activities that bring you joy, such as painting or dancing. You leave early for places that you need to be, so you don't get frustrated easily when time slips by. You make choices that enable peace to blossom. And that is the trick. To consciously choose your desired vibration in every activity. When having difficulty deciding, ask what your manifested self would do. What would peace do? What would love do? What would someone who is successful do? Use affirmations in your daily life to lead the way forward.

When we recite affirmations, we ignite the first step to truly receiving this blessing in our life. The more we speak our desires out loud, the clearer our intention becomes, and the sooner we receive them. We need to tell the Universe, our spirit guides, our angels and ancestors what it is that our soul craves so that they know how best to support us. We need to actively play a role in our life so that we can receive the greatest rewards and live the most fulfilling life.

You are the key character in your life, and you need to remember this truth with confidence and certainty. The best way to do this is by building a strong connection with your soul in the unseen realms, while holding complete faith and trust in the Universe around you. We can do this by speaking words of love to ourselves and those around us. We can do this by embodying our truth through sound energy, by using positive affirmations to describe our current gratitudes in our life and the desires we wish to attain. And most importantly, we can build an unbreakable bond with our soul in the unseen realms by getting to know ourselves wholeheartedly. And we can achieve all of these things through the repetition of spiritual practices.

I AM ALWAYS CONNECTED TO THE DIVINE

PHOEBE GARNSWORTHY   I AFFIRM MY POWER

I am aligned with my higher self.
My energy is calm.
My intuition is clear.
I open my heart to hear the voice of my soul
as I feel its blessings nurture me with love.
Everything in my life now makes sense.
Everything that has been was meant to be.
And I breathe with ease,
knowing that my soul is guiding me forward
with safety and compassion,
with honor and with grace.
I am walking toward my greatest destiny.
I am divinely guided by the Universe at all times.

Creating Your Sacred Space

Do you have a place in your home where you can honor your soul? Do you take time to yourself to give gratitude to all that you have achieved? Have you ever praised all of your talents, intelligence, wisdom, beauty, and gifts? This is the purpose of having a sacred space—to create a shrine of devotion to your soul, to honor your life, and to connect with the spirit world to receive wisdom and manifestations.

The secret to living a fulfilled and meaningful life is to make choices with confidence and to flow with the challenges that we are faced with, as opposed to going against them. The entry point to living a lifestyle that you are proud of starts with learning how to love the person you really are. And to love who you are requires getting to know yourself profoundly. Who are you? And what do you wish to create in this life? To find these answers, you must spend time alone connecting with your soul and learning the truth about your existence. You need to become comfortable with yourself through accepting yourself, both your beauty and flaws. Be self-aware of your limitations, be curious to search how you can improve, and self-reflect over what you aspire to become. You need to learn how to love yourself, and how to listen to yourself. When you are able to achieve all of these things consistently, your soul will be guiding you steadily along your pathway, enabling your life to flow freely and harmoniously in alignment with the magical workings of the Universe.

To honor my soul, I like to create a sacred space where I can peacefully interact with my soul. It is a shrine-like area in my home filled with my favorite things. In this space you can give yourself love, honor, and care. And the more you practice doing this, the more rewards you will reap. In your sacred space you can journal, draw, sing, chant, meditate, and do anything else that makes you feel good. That is the purpose of your sacred space—to gift yourself "you time" and to experience a state of pure bliss with spiritual energy.

To set up your sacred space, you need to:
1) Find a space
2) Decorate your space
3) Create your rituals

1) Find a space

Creating your sacred space doesn't require a lot of work or expense. It can be created at home, with ordinary tools you will find around your house. It can be made in a tiny box, or on a windowsill. All it requires is a place where you can come back to again and again, and in that space you can remember how beautiful and divine you are. Choose a space in your home that can be just yours. If you do not have a space for this, find a box and pack and unpack it as needed.

2) Decorate your space

Call upon the Universe's elemental energies that surround you to decorate your space. These are Earth, Air, Water, Fire, and Spirit. Find anything tangible that represents these energies to you. I will give you some examples of what can be used and also what each of these elements provides to you.

Earth energy will provide you with nurturing love from Mother Nature, deep grounding, and stability. Think: "Mother Nature's gift of harmony." To represent Earth energy, some suggestions could be crystals, a stone or rock, some dirt, a plant, or an ornament that represents or reminds you of Earth.

Air energy gives you clarity over your life, a fresh perspective, and cleansing vibrations. Think: "The breath of life." To represent Air energy, you could use incense, essential oils, a feather, or a figurine that reminds you of air.

Water energy calms your emotions and provides you with ease and fluidity of your thoughts. Think: "Flow with the currents." To symbolize Water energy, you could use a shell, some sand, a small jar of water, or anything symbolic that reminds you of water.

Fire energy has the ability to transform everything. It is protective and strong. Think: "Feed it to the Fire." To represent Fire energy, you could use a piece of wood, a candle, some charcoal, obsidian crystal, something red or yellow, or anything that reminds you of fire.

Spirit energy resides within every living element in the Universe. It is the source of creation and has the ability to love, protect, and guide you. Think: "Spirit is always with me." To represent Spirit energy, you could use a photo of yourself, a drawing, a letter, an angel ornament, or crystals. Anything that represents Spirit energy to you.

If you wish to learn more about these elements, I explore them in depth in my book *Align with Soul*.

3) Create your rituals

A ritual is simply the act of doing something that supports an intention. Your ritual can be as elaborate as you wish, or a simple prayer to yourself. All that is required is dedication to your goals. The more you practice your rituals, the deeper your connection with your soul will become. To create a ritual, you need a sacred space, an intention, and an action. We will explore the magic of rituals in more detail in the next chapter.

Igniting Your Ritual

A ritual is an action that you do repeatedly with the hope to attain something. A spiritual ritual is a sacred act of honor between you and the spirit world performed to achieve something that you desire. Most often, our spiritual rituals are used to call in manifestations, to ask for miracles, to heal, or to release particular energies and pain. When we partake in rituals, we hold hope for something to change, and we know that since we are made of energy, in order for something to change, our energetic vibrational frequency needs to change.

When making your own ritual, all you need are three things:
    1) Your sacred space (an area that honors your soul)
    2) Your intention (what you hope to achieve)
    3) An action (an activity that supports your intention)
Combine these three things, and you can create any ritual that you desire.

To commence your ritual, set up your sacred space and open your ceremony to create a connection with the spirit world. State your intention clearly, either in your mind or by speaking it out loud. If you hope to call in a particular energy—such as peace, love, or healing vibrations—you also need to visualize that energy coming to you. We then use our spiritual tools to support that intention (this is our action). We can do this through many techniques, such as journaling, meditation, or a physical activity. When you feel ready to close your circle, thank the Universe and any spirits or energies that you communicated with. And just like that, you have created a spiritual ritual.

The process of your ritual can vary greatly. I like to set up my sacred space by calling in the Universal energies of creation: Earth, Air, Water, Fire, and Spirit. Each of these energies holds a particular gift for you, and as you become more comfortable with their blessings it will feel more natural for you to call upon their presence to support you in your goals. After this, you may want to create a symbolic gesture to say that you are opening up a passageway to communicate with the Universe. These actions show your desire to interact with the unseen realms. I like to do this through lighting a candle, ringing a bell, or burning some incense or dried herbs. There is no right way to start your ritual. You hold the power to choose how to honor your soul, so allow yourself to move in whatever direction feels right.

To ignite my ritual, I open up my space by saying the following incantation. While doing so, I touch each object and connect with its energy. I also like to create rituals visually, not just with props in reality. And I would do this by reciting my following incantation whilst imagining each energy vibrantly. For example, when referring to Fire energy, I might imagine a blazing sun or fire before me. When talking to Water energy, I might take a sip of water or dip my finger in the water and touch my third-eye chakra to symbolize the purification upon me. Allow your soul to move through your body and guide you. An example of my incantation is as follows:

Fire Energy

I call upon the energy of Fire—blazing light of pure brilliance. May you illuminate the pathway before me so that I may ask for . . . (insert intention).

Water Energy

I call upon the energy of Water—soothing harmony and peace. May your water flow freely around me and within me, calming my emotions and providing me with ease so that I may achieve . . . (insert intention).

Earth Energy

I call upon the energy of Earth—nurturing love and supportive Mother. May I walk confidently upon your path. Please ground my soul within my body as I receive . . . (insert intention).

Air Energy

I call upon the energy of Air—clarity and strength. May your lightness of being breeze through my mind and provide me with the understanding needed to see the answers within for me to . . . (insert intention).

Spirit Energy

I call upon the energy of Spirit—divine source energy of creation. Come forth and bless this space, and send me the wisdom to learn how to . . . (insert intention).

If you would like to call upon your spirit guides, angelic energy, or ancestors, now is the time to do so. I also like to ask Grandfather Sun and Grandmother Moon to come forth so I can thank them for their blessings. The masculine and feminine energy attached to the energies of creation can be traced back to the Indigenous tribes around the world. Personifying the Universal energies of creation with a spiritual essence can be traced back even further, to the ancient Egyptian civilizations. All modern understanding of spiritual energy and magical workings are heavily influenced from the primitive beings of creation.

Once you have opened up your sacred space and ignited your connection with the spirit realm, speak your intention out loud or in your mind. Your intention for your daily rituals will be the affirmation when following this book. After you speak your affirmation, read the definition and follow through with the journaling exercises. Try to be as open and honest as you can. Once you finish, sit and meditate with the meditation prompts. Both of these spiritual tools will be your action that supports the creation of your affirmation to manifest. You can spend as long as you need exploring these practices and sitting in your ritual space.

When you have finished the ritual, close the space by giving gratitude to the Universal energies around you. Symbolize that the ritual has closed, either with words or an action. There are no rules because you are the creator of your life; allow your soul to guide you. All that is asked is to give gratitude and be open to the wisdom laid out before you.

MY SACRED SPACE

PHOEBE GARNSWORTHY

I Affirm My Power

In my sacred space, I harness the energies of the Universe,
as the veil to the spirit world lies thin.
I close my eyes and open my hands to receive its blessings.
And in return, I give them gratitude and praise for all they do.

In my sacred space I connect back with source energy,
to the nurturing place from where I really belong.
I feel the truth of my soul's divinity
as I dance amid the vibration of the Universe's song.

And in this space, I hear the voice of my soul speaking loudly.
I feel the energy of my spirit guides and guardian angels, shining through.
They are all protecting me on my journey here.
They want me to know I will be forever guided too.

And the more I travel in this silent space, the more confident I become.
The more peace, the more love, the more relaxed I feel.
Because this is where my soul breathes freely.
This is my sacred space, where I can be me.

Journaling to Spirit

Journaling is a powerful tool that connects you with the spirit realm. When applied properly and practiced often, journaling gives you the ability to tap into the abundance of wisdom that surrounds you in this life, your past lives, and future generations. You are always connected to source energy, which holds the blueprint of your destiny and the history of your past and present. Therefore, in this energy lies the wisdom to answer all of the questions that you seek. All you need to do is practice connecting to this wisdom, and be open to listening to what it has to say. The guidance you seek is then delivered to you through your intuition by the voice of your soul.

Your intuition is an energy pathway that connects your soul to this reality and the unseen realms together. Through your intuition you have the ability to channel wisdom, access infinite power, and call in or release any energetic vibrations. And journaling assists you in doing this by creating a communication tool for your soul to speak through to you. Not just your soul but also spirit guides, angels, and ancestors—they can all tap in to this energy field and communicate with you.

You are divinely guided by angelic energy at all times. Your soul, along with your spirit guides, angels and ancestors are always with you and want to help you on your life path. The more comfortable you become with communicating with them through the spirit world and heeding their guidance, the easier your life will flow. Because of this, we can understand the spiritual philosophical belief that you hold the answer to every question you ask. Because you have the ability to tap into the unseen realms, into source energy to receive the wisdom from your soul and your spirit guides.

To practice speaking to these energies, come into your sacred space, ignite your ritual, and simply write, without controlling it, by allowing your pen and paper to take over. This is where your soul will channel through your intuition into the spirit realm, to deliver you the message that you need to hear today.

Journaling requires practice and silence. In order for the voice of your soul to speak clearly to you, you need to be open, comfortable, and respectful of your own energy. If you don't feel at peace in who you are, journaling is a perfect entry point to get to this space. Because the more you express your thoughts, and open yourself to receive guidance, the more confident you will become in yourself, your life, and your body. We need to release all the negative energy in our mind to let our soul speak clearly to us, and that is how journaling can support you. By enabling a creative outlet for you to express anything that no longer serves who you wish to be, or become.

To journal: Find space where you can be alone and start by expressing how you feel. Write down the thoughts that confuse you, hold you back, or suppress your ability to be yourself. Relay the emotions you feel and give those emotions a voice to be released as you clarify any questions surrounding them. This is a key component of self-reflection. As you write your thoughts down, you are releasing your energy and asking for new energy to come forth. This new energy can be channeled by simply writing a question and immediately replying. Trust that the answer holds the wisdom from the unseen realms. Don't control the answer; simply write without thinking. You will find that with time you will begin your journaling with the answers already in place, giving you nurturing love and advice upon immediate practice.

In this book, I provide you with journaling prompts to assist your affirmation in cementing itself into your energy field. But you can of course always create your own journaling prompts by simply exploring your thoughts and feelings. The questions that you hold for the Universe, feed them to your soul and see what you receive. The more you practice this sacred session, the louder the voice of your soul becomes, thus creating an unbreakable bond of your intuition and a strong communication channel with the spirit realm.

Journaling was my first spiritual tool for personal transformation. I found deep peace and healing through communicating with my soul, and I was astounded with the profound growth and wisdom that erupted because of this. My journaling began at the young age of nine and has continued up to the present day. And it is still my preferred practice to reveal a greater understanding of my spiritual journey. Through journaling I was able to self-reflect over my past mistakes and actions. I was able to reveal the boundaries that existed within me that I was not aware of. In my journaling, I was able to understand myself and remove the imaginary barrier of feeling so alone in this world. Because I had finally found a safe place to converse with the Universe and understand my soul. It has taken me a long time to get to know my soul. It has been an exploration of trial and error, of spiritual awakenings and a breaking of the ego. It has been a long journey of self-destruction, of unraveling beliefs that I thought were true. A never-ending journey to find the real me. And all of it was documented in my journals, providing me a safe place to express myself freely and find the healing that I needed. With time, I refer to these diary entries whenever I need strength, for I can see how different I am compared with that girl back then. And I can give myself praise for the transformation that has taken place even when I feel like I have had none.

With time journaling can give you the confidence and wisdom that you seek. With practice, journaling has the power to cocreate your destiny. For as you write your goals and dreams down, you are speaking with your soul with great clarity. And when you align your energy with your soul and the magical workings of the Universe, you will be able to attain any manifestation that you desire.

Meditation for Inner Peace

Meditation is a spiritual exercise whose purpose is to retrain the attention of your focus. So often in life we believe that our thoughts are driving our actions and decisions. But in actual fact, your soul is in the driving seat, and your thoughts are there to protect it. But sometimes, our thoughts are not providing the best advice. Sometimes, they want to provide you with logical answers or suggestions as to why something may or may not be true. And your brain finds joy in giving those reasons why, even though they may be negative or detrimental to your well-being. Your brain doesn't decipher that a negative thought is bad or that positive thought is good; it merely wants to provide a service, and that service is to solve problems. But life is not a problem to be solved. It is a journey of great transformation, of beautiful, deep emotions and rewarding experiences—some of which come forth at times when we take risks, when we make illogical choices, and when we trust our heart and soul to lead us forward. So, how do we learn to differentiate between our mind and our soul talking? And how do we know which is best for us at this time? Meditation is a spiritual tool that will provide you with that deep inner peace and knowing. When we meditate, we are able to clear the clutter of thoughts that are not needed in our life. When we meditate, we are able to remove any stagnant energy, negative thoughts, or past pain that is holding us back from being our true, beautiful, intelligent, and talented selves. Meditation is your number one tool to provide you with the mental clarity over your life that you desire.

The process of meditation is not difficult, but like everything, it requires consistency and practice. The more you meditate, the deeper your connection with the spirit world will become, and thus, the braver and more confident you will be to take charge of your life.

To meditate: Get into a comfortable position, which can be lying down or sitting up with your back supported against a wall or pillow. Close your eyes gently and start by taking three to five long, deep breaths to bring your energy into a state of complete calmness. From here, you want to simply observe your energy around you and within you. Notice any feelings of discomfort or blockages, and use your breath to help relax and ease your energy to a state of complete peace. If any thoughts arise during your meditation, do not entertain them; simply accept them and let them go. Focus on cleansing and clearing your energy to be still and unreceptive. You can use your breathing as an anchor to focus your attention or allow your state of peace to be your focal point of awareness. Continue to stay in this position for at least ten minutes.

During this time some people see strong visuals in their meditation practices, others see colors, and some see nothing at all. But regardless of the visualization, there is energy to be felt. You are cleansing, releasing, and renewing your energy field. And since everything in existence is vibrating energy, meditation is a perfect practice to assist you in achieving your personal goals. For you are choosing where to direct your energy, thus removing any thoughts or barriers that are holding you back from achieving your destiny.

My favorite way of meditation is through guided meditation with creative visualizations. These are the kind of meditations that I personally teach, and this is why I have included creative visualization techniques as the meditation prompts in this book. Because we are aiming to embody a particular vibration of our affirmation, in order to support that energy transformation, we can use our imagination as one of the most potent tools. When we visualize our goals, we are embodying the energetic frequency that they already possess, thus calling that energy in abundance into ourselves.

I AM BOTH THE CREATOR AND THE CREATED

PHOEBE GARNSWORTHY

I AFFIRM MY POWER

I stand at the doors of opportunity.

Immersed in the wisdom of the Universe, I see everything clearly.

The world I create around me is not by chance,

it is my destiny.

I hold a blank canvas of infinite possibility.

I glow with divination and seek guidance through this transparency.

My intuition is open and ready to receive the abundance of blessings waiting

for me.

I speak my truth and receive with gratitude.

I live in alignment of my soul and reap what I sow effortlessly.

I am a never-ending cycle of illuminated energy.

Forever expanding, learning, and transforming.

I am creating the life that I crave, for it is my destiny.

I am both the creator and the created,

Whatever I focus my energy on will be delivered to me.

I Affirm My Power

Define: The power within you is endless. It is forever regenerating, renewing, and expanding with every breath that you take. And this power that exists within you is the same power that resides around you. For you are connected to the unlimited abundance of the Universe at all times. You are both the created and the creator. Anything in the entire Universe can be yours, because you have the power to create your life. What you wish to cocreate with the Universe is up to you. But to do so, you need to own that power within. You need to step into the life that you have always desired. Because no one is going to do it for you.

Obtaining this power is not a matter of changing who you are, for you have always held this power. Instead, it is a change of perception of who you think you are. This requires you to own your talents, your intelligence, your beauty; to live your truth; and to believe in your abilities of greatness. You need to remember the infinite power within you that you have carried over many lifetimes. This is the power that your ancestors gave to you. All of that power is wisdom; it's knowledge and intelligence. All of that power is unlimited angelic energy full of love, full of source creation, full of the ability to create the life that you crave and to become the person you aspire to.

Whatever you choose to place your time into, whatever vibration you allow yourself to move to, is where your heart will follow, so be sure to choose wisely. And ensure that it is the truth of what your soul is craving. Because you are powerful regardless of being consciously or unconsciously aware of it. But if you recognize your worth, if you own your gifts and light, if you start stepping into your true power, you will be unstoppable in achieving your goals and calling manifestations into your life.

Today, step into your power. Take a step forward into the real you, into the you that you have been hiding. Remember how divinely guided and loved you are. And that this love that surrounds you wants you to be yourself. Today, affirm your power with your voice, actions, and thoughts. Remember who you really are.

Remember the truth of your own divinity. Remember the power that you have acquired over many lifetimes. You are a marvelous creation of source energy, a vibrant light of pure peace. You are powerful beyond comprehension. And in this power is your ability to be whomever it is that you wish to be, to live the life that you desire. Today is the day to affirm your power.

Journaling Exercise:

Do I believe in my power? Why? Why not?
How can I remind myself of the power within me?
What activities enable my power to soar?
What environments bring forth the greatest loving vibrations within me?
How can I make decisions with confidence from my power?

Meditation:

Close your eyes and bring your awareness to your heart center. Envision a golden ball of energy in this space and spend time defining it clearly. Feel the beautiful softness that this light entails, yet the magnitude of power it possesses. Continue to breathe steadily, slowly in and out as you attempt to grasp the incredible abundance of love that you hold. Now imagine this golden ball of light is expanding and covering your entire body. Let this golden light envelope you in a beautiful cocoon of love and light energy. Feel the power of your own soul as it thrives in this space. You are growing strength, confidence, and peace at this moment. Now, allow this golden light to expand past your body, past your house, and past your city. Let it continue to slowly expand as it soaks up all the power and energy that surrounds you. Allow yourself to melt into this golden light as it continues to expand past the Earth and into the galaxy. Feel the weight of this abundance as it continues to expand as far as it needs to go. Sit here in this beautiful glowing light energy as you feel the beauty of what it truly encompasses. This is your power. Take it.

My Inner Peace Is Strong and Resilient; Nothing Can Shake It

Define: Your inner peace is the entry point to your perception of the world around you. No matter what challenge or grief you may face, if your inner peace is balanced, then there will be nothing that can break it. Because when your inner peace is strong, you have ultimate confidence in yourself and clarity in your life purpose and your presence of being on this Earth. When your inner peace is strong, you are clearly aligned with your soul and have unshakable trust in the Universe. Your inner peace is your rock of faith that holds everything together. It connects your soul with the Universe and brings the wisdom from the unseen realms, from angelic energy, through your intuition channel, and into your reality. If ever the world crumbles around you and your inner peace is strong, you will withstand any storm.

However, strengthening your inner peace takes time and persistence. It isn't something that you can master once; it is something that you must continue to work on over and over again throughout your life. The more time you spend working on your internal self, the greater the voice of your soul, your intuition, becomes—thus providing you with great clarity over your life as you create a harmonic flow of energy between your mind, body, and soul. To practice strengthening this connection will require you to partake in spiritual activities that provide a solid foundation of self-love, self-acceptance, and self-care for you to build upon. Once you learn what activities bring forth the greatest version of yourself, keep practicing them as you build your confidence, and from here, your inner peace will naturally blossom.

If you find yourself getting upset easily over trivial matters that shouldn't be requiring such deep emotional ties, have a look within yourself and see how strong your inner peace is. Have a look within to see how clear and open your communication channel with your soul is, and take some time out of your day to work on yourself through your chosen self-love and self-care activities.

Strengthening your inner peace is achieved through spending time alone. The voice of your intuition is amplified when you honor your soul with activities that illuminate your energy. Listen to your soul and learn what you need to do to build the trust between you. You are always being guided with love by the voice of your soul. The more you align your presence with positive and loving energy, the louder that voice will become. Your inner peace is attainable to you right now at this moment. And know that once your inner peace is created, it will never break; it will only become stronger over time.

Journaling Exercise:

How strong is my inner peace today?
What activities can I do to strengthen my connection to my soul?
How can I listen to my intuition more?
Do I act according to the voice of my intuition? Why? Why not?
How can I have more faith in the magical workings of the Universe?

Meditation:

Bring your awareness to your heart center and imagine it as a glowing gold circle of energy. With every inhale, imagine the gold circle growing bigger. And as you exhale, let it retract back to your heart center. Feel the energy and strength as the circle grows with each breath. Keep allowing this golden light to expand bigger and wider with more brilliance as you inhale and exhale steadily. Immerse yourself completely in this golden light of nurturing love and resilience as you continue to breathe slowly and gradually. Allow this light to completely consume your entire essence. Your every thought, action, and being is molding deeper into the natural vibrations of the Universe. Become one with its love. Sit in this sacred space for as long as you like. This is your armor of protection; it is your inner peace that you are strengthening. If you see or feel any areas that need to be removed or clarified, do so in this space. Create your inner peace to be the beautiful existence that it should be.

The Love I Give Reflects the Love I Receive

Define: What type of love are you seeking today? Are you looking for praise? Recognition? Or a soul-mate relationship? Whatever you wish for, ask yourself, "Am I giving these energies to myself first?" Because whatever you hope to attract, you must first possess it entirely. And then, you will see that the love you crave will magnetically come to you.

If you wish to attract a soul mate, be your own soul mate first. Be the most loyal, respectful, and loving companion to yourself so that you emit the energy first. This is how you will teach others the level of respect and love that you deserve. Too often we hold a fable idea in our head that finding our soul mate completes us, and that it will create a happy life. When, in fact, this isn't entirely true. Because you are already whole and worthy of creating a miraculous life on your own. Finding a soul mate has the ability to complement your life, but it is never a necessity, for you can live a truly rewarding and successful life without one. However, to love and be loved by your soul mate can be a beautiful addition to your already fruitful experience on this Earthly plane. Remember, soul mates come into your life through more than just romance. Unconditional love and loyalty can be found through our family, friends, and animals. If any person or creature comes to mind as you read this, reach out to that soul mate today and tell them they are appreciated and loved.

If you find yourself not believing in your worth, yet you are craving for another to tell you praises, know that it will never be received until you give it to yourself first. You may hear the words that you wish to receive, but because your self-love is low, you will not listen or believe it to be true. So today, you must let go of the limiting belief that you are unworthy and choose to embody the love that you desire. Let go of any fears or worries that are holding you back from receiving this love and step into the confidence and truth of your divine self. Learn how to honor yourself with admiration and high vibrations and use this energy to lead the way forward for others to follow.

Your very essence is filled with the purest and most angelic form of love to ever exist. You are incredibly beautiful, talented, unique, and caring. You are aligned with the abundance of love that surrounds you. You are that love; remember it. Peel away any layers that are holding you back from believing in your ability to receive love. Start by giving yourself love lavishly, and watch how the whole Universe reflects your actions by feeding you with an abundance of blessings in return.

Journaling Exercise:

How do I truly feel about myself?
Do I love myself?
How do I give love to myself?
What activities give love to me, and do I prioritize them?
Do I praise myself?
Do I trust that I am worthy of receiving love?
How can I ensure that I believe in my worth?

Meditation:

Imagine that you are looking at yourself in a mirror. Spend time defining this version of yourself. Clearly outline your beautiful features and, while doing so, give yourself love and praises. Spend extra time on any areas of your face or body that you find yourself having difficulty giving love to. Stay with that feature until you feel peace and love from doing so. Next, focus on the energy that you radiate, and see it as a glowing light that illuminates the space. Allow your energy to glow brilliantly, brightly, and lovingly without any hesitation or restriction. If you find that your energy is dull or patchy, re-create it to be as you wish. Use your intention to create your energy to be however you desire. Make it bright, vibrant, and full of love. Immerse yourself in this beautiful glowing light for as long as you wish.

My Life Flows in Harmony

Define: Sometimes the pathways of our life moves in ways that we cannot possibly understand. We may want it to flow a certain way, and when it doesn't, we stop in our tracks, unsure of how to move forward. Today, whatever is going on in your life, be at peace with it. Surrender into the mystery of the unknown and trust the process. Choose to align with the love of the Universe and believe that all is as it should be.

Whatever you are feeling right now, accept it. Allow any fears, worries, or stress to simply melt away as you take a deep breath and remind yourself that you are divinely guided and looked after by the Universe at all times. If you hold yourself back from surrendering to the magical workings of the Universe, you will find yourself in pain, for you are resisting the truth of your reality. Rather, choose to find peace by accepting yourself and your life right at this moment. Work and flow with the tides of change, instead of pushing against it. This simple change of perception is how you will take your power back. Your new understanding could be: "I am not where I want to be, but I accept that this is where I need to be right now." For when we hold this change of perception, we allow our energy to flow.

If you find your life path to be difficult and uncomfortable, make a different choice to encourage the change that you seek. Or if that is not possible, choose to surrender to what is. Immerse yourself in the wild vibrations of your life journey while holding the ultimate trust and faith that all is meant to be. Find the inner strength within you to persevere in times of confusion. Your journey is unique and full of surprises. If it were to be predictable, you would never experience such profound depths of emotion or transformation. That is what all challenges provide you—an incredible transformation of your soul. You may think you don't want this, but it was written before you entered the Earthly plane. It is all meant to be. And so, you will triumph over it, with success in your favor.

Know that the answers will come through to you soon. Know that the more time you spend honoring yourself and your life path, the easier it will be to flow with the fast-moving pace of changes that you may venture. We are forever faced with hurdles and obstacles throughout our life because these challenges are what enable us to grow and evolve into greatness. If we aren't successful in growing from our difficulties, we will continue to face the same challenge over and over again until we are. Be open to learning how to mold into the new vibration before you to create the changes that you seek. There is nothing that you can't handle. Every challenge is there to create strength and wisdom. Today, surrender into the pain, into the change, into the unknown and allow your energy to flow with the tides of life.

To encourage your life to flow with ease, you need to accept yourself in this moment. Repeat the following affirmation: "I accept myself in this moment. I am at peace with who I am, and where I am going. My life flows in harmony."

Journaling Exercise:
Reflect on your life and identify where you are feeling stuck in your daily path. Start your sentence with the following:
Today, I release the need to ...
Today, I accept ...
What can I let go of today in order to find balance?

Meditation:
Imagine yourself standing at the edge of a lake. There is water flowing gently in front of you. Take your time to enter the lake and allow the water to continue to stream fluidly along its way. As you connect with the energy of water, imagine the cleansing sensation that it provides. Surrender any worries or fears into the water while doing so. Stay immersed in the water, continuously allowing your energy to be cleansed and rejuvenated. If you find your mind drifting while allowing the water to move through you, repeat the following affirmation in your mind: "My life flows in harmony." Stay in the water until you feel yourself immersed in complete peace. As you exit the water, you will feel replenished and revitalized.

I Embrace Any Challenges
Laid Out Before Me

Define: Your life is always flowing according to the divine time. Your soul, before it entered the Earthly plane, chose the best life lessons that you needed to endure in order for great wisdom to bless your soul. The wisdom that you will gain from overcoming such challenges has the ability to change the energetic frequency of your soul's vibration forever. And with each challenge that you overcome, you will receive more grace and wisdom. In order to receive this wisdom, you need to lean in to these feelings of difficulty or inadequacy, while having faith that you are held in the divine love of the Universe. Hold trust in the power of your soul and remind yourself that you are never alone.

You will never face a challenge that you cannot overcome successfully. Each difficulty that is laid out before you was cocreated with the Universe by your soul before you were born. Therefore, every choice in your life is there for a reason. You chose this life. You chose this path, these triumphs, these challenges. It's all there for one reason, and that reason is to enable profound growth within your soul and spirit. Each challenge that you face holds an invitation to change your perception. And with each fraction of your perception that changes, a new understanding of yourself and your life is created. Most often this understanding will be accompanied by wisdom and compassion. Compassion for yourself and others. For you will see that the differences between one another are minute compared with the big picture. Make choices and decisions that you wish for others to make too. Be ethical in your actions, for together we are weaving our life path into the cosmic web of the Universe. And every action and choice that is presented to us has a knock-on effect with each other. As we make more choices that honor the collective, we will, in turn, honor ourselves.

Today, remind yourself of the strength you hold to overcome this heartache, pain, or chaos. Find the spiritual tools that bring you confidence and courage to persevere in times of darkness. And most importantly, be gentle with yourself as you navigate these unknown waters to find the solution that will benefit the evolution of your soul. With each step forward allow your soul to guide you. The whole Universe believes in you. Your angels are sending their blessings to you. They are giving you the strength to persevere and move through these difficulties in your life. Open your heart to believe by feeling the love of your soul within you and use that power to enter with grace any challenge that comes your way.

Journaling Exercise:

What difficulty am I currently facing for which I lack the strength to persevere? How can I find that strength within?
What advice does my soul have for me to overcome this challenge?
What can I do today to support myself?
What strengths do I already hold to face this current challenge?

Write down words of encouragement as you channel your light-warrior self, and trust that these words of positivity are coming from your soul.

Meditation:

Envision yourself as a light warrior covered with beautiful armor to protect you and help you combat any situation in your life. Feel the strength of your ancestors by your side, as each challenge that has been won before you has slithered itself into your own skin. As you imagine yourself in this powerful position, call upon any angels or curious spirits who are able to give you strength as well. Ask for the guidance that is needed and trust the voice of your intuition. Feel the magic of the entire Universe by your side and within your heart as you draw upon its energy. Recite the affirmation in your mind: "I embrace any challenges laid out before me."

I Have Healed Myself in My Dreams

Define: Today, you have awoken with peace in your being and tranquility in your mind. Because while you were asleep, you journeyed to the unseen realms and heeded the wisdom from your ancestors who have passed. While your mind and body were sleeping deeply, your soul rested in the sacred waters of divine love. Here in this space of healing vibrations, you received the answers to any problem that you currently face.

Your dreams create a safe space for you to heal. Because during this time your soul is visiting the angelic realms with your spirit guides, and you are guided by your Higher Self to find the solutions to all of your problems.

While you were asleep, your soul explored the spirit realms. You sought wisdom and received healing light from the angelic entities who support your growth here on Earth. In this space, your soul is connected to the abundance of Universal energy that surrounds you. While you are sleeping, your consciousness is able to rest. And this enables you to tap into the unseen realms without any interference of thought or mind. You are free to gain wisdom, clarity, and strength. In this sacred space, you mold back into the vibrations of the Universe's creation. You come home to your true self. Back to the sacred space of spiritual cosmic intelligence. This is where you come from. And all of your ancestors, your spirit guides, and angelic beings are here with you, as they help you to create harmony in your life.

When you are ready to leave this space, you return to the Earthly plane refreshed and revived. Your energy is now completely nourished, nurtured, and rejuvenated. You embody health with a vibrant glow of pure radiance, for you have healed your wounds as you have slept. You have turned your scars into wisdom. That wisdom is your power. You now hold the ability to see through the darkness laid out before you. And here you can make choices and changes in your life with the confidence you have been craving.

You hold complete clarity over your problems, for you have gained the answers while you were asleep, and only blessings are coming to you now. Only positive vibrations and loving energies are on their way. You are loved, blessed, and divinely guided by the Universe. You have healed yourself in your dreams.

Journaling Exercise:

Keep a journal next to your bed as you sleep. Write down any questions or problems that you need the solutions to before you go to sleep. In the morning write down the first thing that comes to you when you awake. Have a look over the memory of your dreams. Recall any symbols or experiences and write down what they mean to you—literally and emotionally. Ask yourself what the answer is for your problem. Write down the first thing that comes to you, and trust that the right answer has been received.

Meditation:

This meditation is to help you go to sleep.

Anchor your presence by slowing your breathing down to a steady rhythm. After several minutes of deep breathing, imagine a stairwell reaching up high into the galaxy. Walk up this stairwell very slowly. With each step invite in peace and harmony, tranquility, and love while you sleep. Set your intention again and ask for any answers needed for your current struggle. Tell yourself that you will awake with the answer. When you reach the top of the stairwell, stand there, and continue to focus on your breath as you wait to be taken away into your peaceful dreams to seek the wisdom that you desire.

I Always Trust the Divine Timing of My Life

Define: Everything in your life is as it should be. Everything in your life is right on time. You don't need to worry about a thing. Whatever has happened is behind you now. And it was meant to have happened. So, hold peace in knowing that.

Today, leave all your stress and pain behind. Let go of any expectations or limiting beliefs that are holding you back from being true to yourself. Know that you are walking in alignment with your Higher Self and that everything laid out before you is crucial to the fulfillment of your destiny. All of your challenges and hardships have been necessary to endure so that you may fulfill your soul contract.

Your soul contract holds a series of life lessons that enable the energy of your soul to evolve into greatness. With every difficulty that you overcome, great wisdom is received. And because of this belief, we know that everything laid out before us is there for a reason. Every happiness, pleasure, sadness, and grief holds an opportunity for transformation, and that transformation has the ability to change our perception of the world forever.

If you find yourself uneasy with your life and wish for something to change, what you actually need is a change of perception. We hold the tools within us to live the life that we crave, to build the inner peace that we depend on, and to live our lives with the freedom that we deserve. Look within and find your desired spiritual tool to help you trust the divine timing of your life. This tool could be an activity of self-love or self-care, or it may simply be a moment of strength needed to overtake your mind. A moment to say to yourself, "I accept where I am in my life right now, and I let go of any expectations." Today, accept and surrender into the unknown. Simply let go of what was, what is, and what will come.

Instead of allowing yourself to feel suffocated with this challenge, embrace this knowing of oneness with the Universe and find the peace from such trust. Embrace your faith in the unknown. Spend time alone with your soul to hear the wisdom of your spirit guides as you remember the truth of who it is that you really are—a divine creation of the Universe's love. You haven't lost time. You don't need to be anywhere else than where you are right now. Because everything is and has always been right on time. Trust the divine timing of your life and know that everything that is being gifted to you at this moment is exactly what is meant to be. Honor your truth, honor your life path, and honor your faith in the magical workings of the Universe.

Journaling Exercise:

What is holding me back from trusting my life path?
What expectations have I placed upon myself to "be" somewhere else?
What do I find difficult to accept in my life?
How can I overcome this fear?

When looking at these thoughts, challenge them with your new attitude of acceptance of the present moment: "I am right where I need to be. I always trust the divine timing of my life."

Meditation:

Lie down on the ground and feel the Earth supporting you. Close your eyes as you breathe in and out deeply in alignment with the natural vibrations of Mother Nature. Let those vibrations soothe your mind, your body, and the energy of your soul. Allow your body to become very heavy as you sink deeper into relaxation. Feel your energy weigh deeply into the cocoon of Mother Nature's love. In this safe space, surrender any fears, thoughts, or grief into the Earth and allow yourself to become "as one" with the Universe. Surrender into its love. Repeat your intention clearly in your mind until you believe it with unshakable trust: "I always trust the divine timing of my life."

I Am Whole on My Own

Define: There is no need to search outside of yourself, for everything that you have ever wanted is already within you. Your soul vibrates amongst the frequency of angels, and in this space it radiates with the purest form of love that ever existed. Your energetic vibration exudes the most profound wisdom and vitality. And in your physical being you encompass beauty, intelligence, and optimal health. Your talents are endless. Your resilience is unbreakable. You have the courage and strength to overcome any challenge that comes your way. There is no need to seek outside for wholeness from another, for you have always held an abundance of pure love within. The entire Universe believes in your divine existence in the human world, on the Earthly plane, and now it's time for you to believe in it too. The moment you choose to align your beliefs with the powerful truth of who you really are is the moment you will feel the complete wholeness of perfection that you seek.

You hold both light and darkness within you. But neither side is good nor bad; rather, it's the definition you choose to place upon them. Both together make a whole, and both sides are needed for balance and harmony. It is you who must use your perception of these two entities to support your choices here on the Earthly plane. If you find yourself leaning more to one side than the other, recognize when this happens and readjust accordingly. Remind yourself that this is merely an illusion of your own existence. For you always embody the ability to be at peace within yourself between these two vibrations. It's just a matter of mastering your mind and emotions to calm yourself. The ideal presence is to be in a state of peace from a harmonious marriage of the two entities. And this can easily be achieved by finding your inner peace and opening your heart to feel the energy of your soul vibrating in the angelic realms as you step into your truth of oneness with the Universe.

Remember your power within. Remember your ability to choose which side you wish to nurture. Remember that it is up to you to believe in your talents, to believe in your worth, and to believe in yourself. You have always been enough, from the moment you existed. You are loved by the whole Universe because you are an extension of the Universe's love and its creation. You are completely perfect at this moment right now and have always been. You have everything that you need right here on your own.

Journaling Exercise:

Where in my body, mind, and soul do I feel incomplete?
What limiting belief do I hold about myself that is harming me?
What is my story of incompleteness?
Where does it come from?
Where do I lack love for myself?
How can I give that love to myself?
How can I use love for myself to find the solutions that I crave?

Meditation:

Envision the energy of your soul. What do you see? Is it a light, or a feeling? Is it a color, or an emotional vibration? Tune in to that energy and allow it to overtake your senses. Allow yourself to be completely immersed in this beautiful light as you choose to release any stagnant energy that is weighing you down. Continue to breathe slowly as you focus on harmonizing the flow of energy within your mind, body, and soul. Use the energy from the Universal cosmos to support your vision. If you need to cleanse your energy, cleanse it with love from the Earth. If you need to brighten your energy, allow the stars from the galaxy to fall upon you and fill you up with stardust. Continue to feel the pureness of your soul's energy. And if you start to sway from its beauty, bring yourself back into alignment. Know that the love within you is pure, and remind yourself that you are whole and complete on your own.

My Soul Speaks Words of Love through My Intuition

Define: Deep down, you know the difference between your soul and your ego talking. You know the true voice of your intuition loud and clear. But sometimes you get distracted, and the sound of your mind takes over, telling you what "could be" the better thing to do. This can create much confusion and stress in your body because each piece of advice that you are hearing may feel right. One is coming from your mind, and is providing a logical reason. This logical reason may be a safe option and might sound like the right option because it is protecting you. But there is another voice feeding you advice that is coming from your heart, your intuition, your soul, and it is providing you with the guidance to lead the most rewarding and fulfilling experience here in this life. It may feel like the greater risk, and you may look like a fool or fall down, but it is going to give you more wisdom, more confidence, more courage, more understanding, and more compassion for years to come. For when we act from the voice of our intuition, we are encouraging the perception of our mind to expand.

When deciding which voice you should listen to, how do you know which one is that of your intuition? Both may make sense, so ask yourself: "Which voice is coming from love? What advice would bring me the greatest life experience, the highest rewards, and the most profound emotional growth?" Through these simple questions, you will learn how to differentiate between the two. The voice of your ego wants to protect your image to the outside world. It doesn't care about the spiritual growth that you could attain from making certain life choices, whereas the voice of your soul will always encourage you to live authentically and to make decisions that bring out the best in you. Taking risks and leaps of faith in the Universe is what life is all about. Learning to listen to the voice of your soul, to your intuition, is a skill that you need to practice and strengthen.

Your soul's purpose is to guide you through the most unbelievable life experiences with deep, raw emotion. If you choose to dismiss the voice of your intuition, the voice of your soul will become weak and faint. The more you practice listening to your soul, talking with your soul, and becoming friends with your soul, the easier your life will flow. Your soul will always speak words of love. It will always encourage you to live a life rich with flavor and excitement. Trust and believe in the power of yourself. The more that you do, the louder the voice of your intuition will become.

Journaling Exercise:
What is the truth that I know deep down within that I have been ignoring?
What is the right answer in alignment with love?
What decision can I make to bring forth deep maturity, growth, and wisdom?
What are some ways that I can connect with my soul more?
What environment does my soul thrive in?
What am I doing to support the voice of my intuition?

Meditation:
Close your eyes and sit with your back supported (either in a chair or against a wall). Start by connecting with the energy of your third-eye chakra (the space between your eyebrows). Envision a beautiful deep-blue light that is projecting from this space outward into the Universe's galaxy. This is your intuition channel. Spend time defining this blue light energy and use your breath to clear any obstructions in its view. Once the energy is clear and open, call in any advice or wisdom that you need to know. Your Higher Self, your spirit guide, your ancestors, angels, or angelic spirits will feed you the knowledge that you seek. Practice strengthening this communication channel as often as possible.

Peace, calm, and collected. This is the energy I choose to feel. This is the energy that I choose to embody. My inner self is in harmony with the vibrations of the universe, and from this space, I flow freely. I am in tune with my rhythm and the cycles of life. I surrender and hold faith in the magical workings of the Universe. And because of this that I hold dear in my heart, I can hear the voice of my soul speaking loudly. "Go closer, lean back, step forward, give them love." It echoes through my heart.

With every breath, I step closer to that radiating light within me. And from this space I breathe with ease, knowing that everything around me is exactly as it should be.

I Create Beauty Everywhere I Go

Define: The way you see the world is unique, wonderful, and truly magnificent. Because of this perspective, you have the ability to create beauty everywhere you go. You are a divine light of angelic energy dancing through your life here on Earth, creating magic and miracles. Everything that you touch has the potential to turn into greatness, because this is how you choose to see it. You aren't being oblivious to the darkness, but you have the ability to find the light within it. Because of this talented gift, you are able to find good in the world that not many people can. Because of this optimism, people love being around you. Your heart is so full and nourished that your empathy for others vibrates high when their life isn't going well. You can always find a way to make others smile, and that is a wonderful gift to hold. The more beauty you embody and share with others, the greater the rewards you will reap as you create the world around you to be the blissful experience of joy that you know so well.

But sometimes you forget to apply that lens of optimism to your own life. You are quick to compare yourself to others, thinking that their life is much more fruitful than your own. And you can spend too much time searching and dreaming of another's life, ignoring the miracles that your own life holds. In times like these, make sure that you come back home into yourself. Use your positive perspective on your own life through gratitude and recognition of all the blessings around you. Don't spend all your time highlighting others' success to a point that it brings you down. Don't feed yourself lies that everyone else's life is perfect, because it's not. Everyone has their own struggles, just as you do. Cheer everyone on, but don't neglect your own life. Stay aligned with your goals. And at times of despair, remind yourself of all that you have achieved, all that you have overcome, and all that you have gained. It's easier for you to shift the attention from your own success onto another, because hidden in the shadows is where you find it more comfortable to be. But it's time to stand strong in your own light and embrace the beauty that is around you and within you. To be beautiful is to create inner peace and happiness with carefully selected words and actions that provide positive ripples into the Universe's energy. Being beautiful is something that is felt through energy, and right now your energy is radiating with glorious bliss.

So today, attune this unique lens of optimism and positivity to your life and rejoice in all the miracles that are laid out before you. Find the good in your life and sing its praises with confidence in knowing that more rewards are coming to you. You are surrounded with beautiful, high-vibrational energies, and those energies are radiating from within you, and for you. Harness those energies today by opening yourself up to see them, and in doing so, you will become them.

Journaling Exercise:

On a scale of one to ten, how beautiful do I feel today?
What is the most beautiful vibration that exists in my life?
How can I harness more of that vibration?
What are some beautiful words I can use to describe me?
How can I bring more beauty into my life?
What acts of kindness show the beauty of my soul?
How often am I spending time cherishing my own divine light within?
What can I do to make a difference in the world around me?

Meditation:

Imagine the most beautiful flower you have ever seen. Envision its color, its petals, and its fragrance in complete detail. Feel the energy that this flower provides you. Feel the vibrations, feel the soothing nature, feel the loving beauty. This flower is representing the beauty within you. Imagine yourself mirroring the energy that the flower emits. See the energy of both you and the flower rising high and vibrating with peaceful vibrations. Then allow the flower to come closer into your aura. Hold the flower tightly and bring it into your heart. As you bring the flower into your energy field, become as one with the flower. Allow yourself to mold together as you align your energy with the beautiful vibrations of the Universe.

I CREATE BEAUTY EVERYWHERE I GO

I see the divine within you.

I see the love you hold within your heart blazing fiercely.

I know your soul is pure.

I know we have walked on this Earth many times together before.

I see you for the true energetic being that you are.

I see your beauty overflowing in every breath of stillness.

You hold great wisdom within your heart.

Your talents are guiding you toward your greatest success.

There is so much goodness within you.

You have so much joy to gift another.

But gift that joy to yourself first.

Send those loving vibrations into your heart first.

And then, the world will open up in ways you have never thought possible.

You will see the illuminated soul of every living creature around you.

And you will connect more deeply, more profoundly,

By simply being your true self,

By living authentically in alignment with who you really are.

And who are you?

A cosmic flame of stardust, dancing through this miraculous dream we call life.

I Live Authentically in Alignment with My Soul

Define: When you live in alignment with your soul, you feel a deep sense of peace within you, for you know that you are living as your most authentic, raw, and truthful self. When you live from this space, your soul is grounded in your body, feeling completely nurtured and nourished from the energy of Mother Nature. When you live in alignment with your soul, you are able to fulfill your life purpose, enabling you to lead a vibrant and rewarding life. When you live in alignment with your soul, you are able to make powerful decisions with confidence, as you now hold complete clarity over your life path. From here, your life flows easily because you know the answers to all of your questions. You hold the ability to act courageously from this space of pure love as you feel the abundance of creation from source energy at the core of your being.

To live from this space, as your authentic self, you first need to reveal what it is that your soul wants from this life. You need to learn about what kind of person you aspire to become, and you need to be crystal clear on your boundaries to protect and support yourself as you achieve your goals in this life. And most importantly, you need to love yourself as you discover the incredible uniqueness of who you are and what you are put on this Earth for.

This raw, truthful, authentic version of yourself is the *real* you. It's the version of yourself that your soul craves, that your soul sings with joy throughout your body. You have the power to be this version of yourself, but so often we are fearful of how incredible and mighty we can become. We don't know how to handle our own power and are afraid to appear as if we are loving ourselves, in case others look down on us for it. But we can't live in fear of what another might think, for then we would be serving another and not ourselves. We need to embrace the truth of who we really are, as we live confidently and bravely in alignment with our soul. The more we live as this version of ourselves, the happier we will become, the more naturally our life will flow, and the more miracles and synchronicities will come our way.

You know the truth of who you really are. You know how to live in alignment as this pure version of yourself. Work through any hesitation within that is holding you back from stepping into this alignment. The moment you choose to be who you desire to be, you will be happy, free, and completely at peace with all that is around you.

Journaling Exercise:

Who is it that I wish to be?
What qualities do I aspire to hold?
What kind of life do I want to live?
What energy do I wish to vibrate?
What wisdom do I seek?
How can I be a better version of myself?
Where do I lack love for myself?
How can I step into this power more?

Meditation:

Imagine yourself as the most beautiful, pure, loving light energy that you can possibly envision. Define this version of yourself carefully. What do you look like? What energy do you radiate? How are you living your life? Envision and feel it. Move your vibration closer to this version of yourself. And then, when you are ready, step into this energy field. Completely embody this vibration as though you, yourself, were exuding it first. Search within to find where you are holding yourself back from believing in its existence. Find the blockages within yourself and breathe that energy out into the Universe. Welcome in new vibrations to take their place. Invite in new vibrations that encompass who you really are. And know that with each breath in and each breath out, you are stepping deeper into alignment with your authentic self.

I AM GROUNDED WITH LOVE

PHOEBE GARNSWORTHY   I AFFIRM MY POWER

Balanced. Calm. Supported. Nurtured. In love with the Earth.

I wandered through the fields of dirt and broken shadows to find true love.

And there it was. But not a person, not an object or a creature, it was an energy.

It was the source of creation.

And in this space of beauty and wisdom, I asked her to heal me. And to love me.

And I threw myself carelessly into the wildness of her arms.

Dancing with freedom around the only space I truly felt at home.

The stones and flowers dispersed before me, I saw the energy that they provided.

The essence of their beauty. The magic of their blessings.

It was within me and around me. I didn't want to leave. I didn't want it to stop.

It was the first time in my life that I felt complete wholeness.

It was the first time in my life that I felt truly alive.

I Am Grounded with Love

Define: When your energy is grounded, your soul is able to thrive through your body, here on Earth. When your energy is grounded, you can make decisions with clarity and confidence, as you live with ease, completely at peace with the present moment. When your energy is grounded, you are able to live your life wholeheartedly with admiration and gratitude, as you now see things clearly around you. In this space, you have the stability to open your heart and mind, encouraging an eagerness to learn and expand as you bring forth new understandings of who you are and what your world contains. When your energy is grounded, you walk in alignment with your Higher Self, hearing the voice of your intuition loudly as it guides you along your life path.

But when we are not in this space, we can feel as if we are drowning in our own world of misery. When we are ungrounded, we hold tightly to fear, and we start to doubt the choices of our life journey. When we are ungrounded, we linger too long on false vibrations, trying desperately to find something to make us feel in control of our life. During this time, our body may feel heavy, unable to move forward as we find ourselves having difficulty letting go of past mistakes or regretful decisions. But all of that chaos that you hold can change in a mere moment just by focusing on grounding yourself. All of those heavy vibrations that are weighing you down can simply melt into the Earth around you, if you want them to. But even the sadness that you feel still needs to be felt in order to let it go, and if your soul is not grounded and you are not present to feel this energy, then it will hover until you do. To move past any pain or stress, we need to feel it, and when we are grounded, we are in a safe space to do so. When we are grounded, we are connected to the energy of the Earth, we are caressed by Mother Nature, and her powerful energy is able to handle anything.

When you ground yourself, you are asking for the love of Mother Nature to help bring your soul back into reality. Together, you call out to your soul in the unseen realms to bring all your energy that has ever been released back into your body. And when you regain your energy, you can live wholeheartedly, open, and ready to experience the depths of emotions that life can bring.

To ground yourself, walk out into nature and let Mother Earth heal your pain. Sit with her beauty and focus on your breathing, as you call all your energy back from wherever you have expanded and gifted it. Allow the pain of your past to melt away into her love, for Mother Nature will heal you, ground you, and bring forth great enlightenment to you. Her love is unconditional. Her love is never-ending. Her love will soothe your soul as you walk with confidence here on Earth by her side.

Journaling Exercise:

Do I feel grounded or ungrounded today?

What problems in my life have arisen because I am ungrounded?

What activities have I done recently that ground my soul into my body?

How often do I ground myself?

What are my favorite ways to ground myself?

When did I last spend time with Mother Nature nurturing my energy?

Meditation:

Sit down with your back supported and your eyes closed. Take deep breaths until you are in a deep state of meditation. Once you are here, imagine you have roots like a tree, growing down from your pelvis into the ground below. Let those roots sink deeply into the Earth and connect with Mother Nature. As your roots enter the Earth, feel her nurturing love supporting you. Allow yourself to feel completely supported as you surrender your divine self into Mother Nature's love. Let the energy from her love soothe your worries and fears. Let the energy of her love bring you peace as you ground your soul back into your body. In this space, call out to your soul and imagine any energy of yours that is floating around you coming back into your heart center. Call that energy back in as you ground your soul into your body once more.

I Have the Power to Achieve My Goals

Define: Those goals that you secretly hold up high in the sky are coming to you. Every single one of them. Why? Because they are your destiny. They were preconceived by your soul before you entered the Earthly plane, and for this reason, they are written into your soul contract. You will achieve all the success that you crave. You will attain the life that you desire, but only if you believe that you are worthy of receiving it. As you create your goals, speak to your soul and ask what it wants. Ask what it craves and then actively work toward those goals every day. For we cannot receive something that we are not actively pursuing.

What are you doing today to achieve your dreams? The first step is believing you are worthy of receiving them, and with that comes confidence. Let go of any limiting beliefs that are holding you back from truly believing in your self-worth. Let go of any fear that makes you think that you cannot attain your dream life, because your goals are predestined for you. The second step is to create changes in your life that have the ability to call those aspirations in. And work on those actions every day, consciously or unconsciously. The final step is to let go of the wanting, because you have an abundance of faith and ultimate trust in the Universe that everything you want is coming. Letting go of your dreams doesn't mean that you are giving up; instead, you can still want those things, but you have already spoken your desires with the Universe, and you are letting go of the need to control it because it's in the Universe's hands now. And you know that the Universe always supports your soul's destiny. Ensure that your actions, words, and events in your life support attaining the goal that you want, so that when the time is right, the Universe can swiftly deliver your desires.

You have unlimited power pulsating through your body, enabling your soul to cocreate your destiny with the Universe. You have the ability to design a life that you desire, all by simply asking, acting, and believing. What is it that you wish for today that you are not believing you are worthy of receiving? Break down those limiting beliefs and unnecessary barriers in your mind that are holding you back from living your truth. Let go of the negative thoughts and empty spaces that are weighing you down and telling you that you are not good enough or worthy of receiving this life that you crave. Because you crave these goals and this success, you will receive them. Everything that our soul craves is destined to be. As you speak your desires out loud, the Universe will magnetize your soul to its future. Your every action is creating the world that you were always meant to be living. Your destiny is everything you have ever imagined it to be and so much more.

Journaling Exercise:
What is my greatest desire for my life?
What does success mean to me?
What vibration does my soul crave?
How can I embody these goals?
Write it down; don't leave any details to spare.
Be as specific as you can be, because this is your moment to converse with the Universe.

Meditation:
Imagine what it would feel like to be living the life that you desire. Envision the energy that you would be giving and receiving in your everyday life. Imagine that your life is as successful as you are dreaming for it to be. Completely allow yourself to vibrate at this high frequency. Allow any fears or questions to arise within your body and mind, but do not entertain them. Instead, let them go and clear that energy with pure, loving light vibrations from the Universe above. Continue to immerse yourself in this high vibrational energy as you lean deeper and deeper into your ultimate goals—until you become completely as one with the Universe. Embody those dreams, hold those desires, and then simply let them go. Stay aligned with complete faith that they will come to you when the time is right.

I Have All the Answers I Need Right Now

Define: Is there a question of uncertainty lingering over your life? Are you unsure about making a decision that could change everything that you've ever known? Trust that you hold the wisdom within you to always make the best choices for your life. Because you do. Your soul knows the true pathway of your destiny. Therefore, you know the answers too. So why are you refusing to believe them? Why are you choosing to ignore the truth? If you were to follow the advice of your soul, you would be gifted incredible transformation. But know that in doing so, you may be required to prove great resilience and strength. But I'll tell you a secret that your spirit guides want you to know: You can do it. You can make the right choice and take charge of creating a life that you love. Because this challenge laid before you was written into your soul contract before you entered this life. And for this reason alone, you will succeed. And when you finally move through this difficult phase, you will transform into the greatest version of yourself ever possible. This transformation is so close to you now; will you take the leap? Lean in a little bit deeper. Open your heart a little bit wider. And let the wisdom of your angels and ancestors pour through into the crown of your head as you carry on with your day with confidence and power. Let your intuition lead the way forward.

There are no wrong choices in life; there's no wrong pathway for you to take. Because everything that is placed in your life is an opportunity to step deeper into a more authentic you. And in return, you will always receive an incredibly rewarding experience. But what you make of that experience is up to you. Saying yes and saying no are both empowering decisions, so either option can be the right choice for you.

Accept yourself right at this moment. Accept where you are and remind yourself that you are divinely guided and looked after by the energies of the Universe. Everything in your life has led you to this great turning point; whether you choose to embark down the pathway before you is your choice alone. If you are waiting patiently for a new pathway to open up, have a look around you. It's there; you just need to see it. Ask yourself what you wish to receive and look within to see what you are doing to make it happen. Your Higher Self, which is your soul in the unseen realms, is supporting you and guiding you, encouraging you to be brave and to take a step forward. The answers you seek are already within you; it's just a matter of peeling back the layers to find them.

Sit with the choices laid out before you. Close your eyes and imagine both options playing out. Feel the energy that they could provide you. And then, go with whatever energy feels better for you. Trust the voice of your intuition to lead you forward.

Journaling Exercise:

What area of my life do I hold confusion over?
What answers am I seeking today?
What advice is my Higher Self giving me?
How do I feel about that advice?

Meditation:

Connect with your intuition to find the answers that you seek. Imagine the energy of your Higher Self in the unseen realms in front of you. Envision a blue cord of energy from your physical body that connects you to your Higher Self. Take your time defining this blue energy cord of communication. If it is weak, stagnant, or has holes in its field, patch them up. Make the energy cord of your intuition strong. Make it thick, fluid, and transparent. And then, when you are ready, talk through this energy field and ask your intuition for the guidance that you seek. Trust in the power of yourself, your Higher Self, and the power of the Universe. Be open to receiving the wisdom before you. Feel the energy of the advice, and when you awake, make your choice.

I Have Brilliant Ideas and the Confidence to Act Upon Them

Define: There are bountiful talents within you. A wealth of unique creativity and intelligence just waiting to be explored. Your soul is itching to reveal its knowledge, but in order for you to hear its voice, you need to own what it has to say. You must love yourself completely to truly praise the gifts that you have been given. And you need to use your gifts to the fullest, by being authentically and unapologetically yourself. When we are our authentic selves, our souls have their chance to fly freely. When we live in alignment with our soul, the most incredible ideas come forth, and our confidence to fulfill those ideas becomes unstoppable. The more we lean into the voice of our soul and dare to believe in ourselves, the brighter our gifts will shine.

You are so talented. You need to use those talents. You have a unique perspective of life, and the whole world craves to learn from you. The moment you choose to align with your soul and live your authentic truth is the moment your life will flow freely and bring forth the most incredible rewards. But sometimes you are scared to listen to your soul. Sometimes you dumb yourself down to fit in or think that no one will like you if you stand out too much—but the world needs you to stand out. Others need you to share your gifts and caring nature so that they will be inspired to do so too. The entire collective consciousness depends on your willingness to be true to yourself, because the more we allow ourselves to shine, the better chance the collective has in ascending and uplifting itself into greatness together.

So today, listen to the truth within your heart. Listen to the voice of your soul. It is calling for you to act upon your ideas. You soul wants you to fulfill your destiny by living the life that you love. This is the life that you deserve. Listen to the guidance of your spirit guides; they know exactly what you need to do to live the life that you are dreaming of. Feel the energy of your divine presence as you experiment with life's experiences. Take note of what activities light up your frequency. And go boldly toward them. Speak your goals out loud to the Universe as you walk confidently toward the direction of your dreams. Show the world your talents. Show them how incredibly gifted you are, and how proud you are to be living this life. Only you can create the life that you desire. Only you can fulfill your life purpose. Your guides will help you, your soul will steer you, but it's up to you to listen, to love, and to be brave. We all believe in you.

Journaling Exercise:

What are my talents?

What am I good at without even trying?

What brilliant ideas have I been thinking about, but have been too scared to act upon?

Am I living as my authentic self, or am I hiding who I really am?

How can I gain the confidence to be my true self?

What can I do today to support my goals and ideas?

Meditation:

Close your eyes. Use your breath to bring yourself into a deep meditative state. Envision the truth of who you really are. See yourself as the divine creation of light energy that you embody. Visualize the abundance of love, talents, and gifts that you hold. See them as colorful lights or feel them as their loving vibrations. As you view this spiritual image of yourself, search within to see what is holding you back from believing this is who you really are. Because this incredible divine light of pure, wondrous joy *is* who you really are. Take your time to step closer and closer to this beautiful version of yourself until you feel it within you, and you feel yourself embody it completely. And when you open your eyes, you will know that you truly are this divine light of angelic energy, destined to create incredible things.

My Emotions Are Valid, and I Welcome Them with Ease

Define: Accept any feelings that are arising within you. Acknowledge their existence and don't resist the depth of their beauty. Your emotions are valid. They are here to teach you something. They are an invitation for wisdom. Because whatever we find uncomfortable in life is actually an opportunity for growth. Your emotions hold a valuable lesson for your life journey. And if you try to suppress or disown them, they will become louder. Just because your emotions may feel strong and overpowering, it doesn't mean that your thoughts and actions are right, or that you need to react abruptly. It just means that there is a gift to be found. Today, look to your feelings for their true meaning of wisdom and guidance.

Your emotions are energy stirring within you. And inside that energy, there is something to be revealed. The pathway to discovering this revelation is through owning your feelings. It's through entering your feelings, no matter how difficult they may be. Ask for protection and safety from your spirit guides and angels. Ask for confidence and courage from your Higher Self as you walk through these emotions. And then, when you are ready, let your feelings have the honor that they deserve by accepting that they are a part of you. Give them a voice. Provide your feelings with a healthy outlet to release their energy. Suggestions of this could be through movement and dance, singing, crying, laughing, or breathing.

Take your time to express yourself and release this energy. Soothe your soul through Mother Nature, or the Universal energies of Water, Air, Earth, Fire, and Spirit. Once the energy has dispersed, new energy can take its place. And inside this new energy, you will find profound wisdom, telling you the reasons why you felt this way. Through this wisdom, you will discover the real message that needs to be heard. Do you need to love yourself more deeply? Do you need to forgive yourself or someone else? Do you need to be more compassionate? Do you need to speak your boundaries more loudly? Whatever the wisdom, trust your intuition to guide your way forward.

Once you have transformed this dark energy into lightness, you will be at peace. The answers and reasons why you felt this way will come through to you clearly. And from here, you can act and speak according to your soul's needs. Ask yourself, "What did that emotion teach me?" And finally, your emotion can rest. Your feelings can subside. For your perception of the world is no longer a clouded judgment of their presence. And you can finally see things clearly, for what they truly are.

Journaling Exercise:

What emotion am I feeling today?
How much of this emotion is controlling my life and daily happiness?
How can I embody this emotion and release it healthily?
Now that I am not consumed in this emotion, what was it here to teach me?
How can I find wisdom from this experience?

Meditation:

In a deep state of meditation, feel the emotion that is consuming you. Allow it to arise within you and overtake your whole body. Sit with that emotion. Truly feel its expression. Ask if there is something to be shown. Allow yourself to become completely absorbed in its presence, and then, when you are ready, release it. Imagine a hole beneath you in the ground, and feed that energy into Mother Nature. Use your breath and imagine that energy falling down into Mother Earth. She will happily consume this energy for you. If you need extra assistance, use your breath to blow the energy out of you as you move your arms with your breath and release it. Or you may feel inclined to cry or shout. Whatever you need to do to release that energy, do it. And once that energy is released, invite in pure, harmonious, and peaceful vibrations. Let Mother Nature serve you with light energy. Once you have awoken from the meditation, write down any messages or guidance that was presented to you.

I Release and Let Go of Anything That No Longer Serves Me

Define: Today is the day to release any stagnant energy that you've been holding on to. The pain in your heart, the sorrow in your gaze, the hurtful memories that are weighing you down, the limiting beliefs and negative thoughts—none of these things have been helping you be your best self, so why not let them go? You have been holding on to these low vibrations because you believed that this is what you were worth. You have been using them as a way to define yourself. But it is not the truth of who you really are. You are so much more powerful than you can possibly comprehend. You are a divine extension of the Universe, filled with an abundance of love and prosperity. You are a miraculous creation of manifested consciousness, and it's time to start owning the truth of who you really are. It's time to step into your true power. It's time to align with your authentic self and start using the gifts that you have been blessed with.

To release this stagnant energy, start by making a conscious choice to do so. Tell yourself that this energy is no longer serving your greatest good and that you wish for new vibrations to take its place. But as you release these feelings, thoughts, and memories, make sure you create new ones. Be an alchemist of your own energy and ignite the changes that you seek. Seek out high vibrations in your life, call them in, and request more blessings from the Universe.

Move your vibration closer to what lights up your soul. Find the activities in your life that bring you joy and do more of them. Because incredible beauty, unlimited talents, intelligent wisdom, and all the success and love you have ever wanted are waiting for you. It is your destiny to live in this space of unlimited potential. But you can't receive any of this while holding on to the past. You cannot live with happiness while holding tightly to fear. So today, transform and transmute these negative vibrations into positive ones by accepting their existence, and then simply letting them go. Find a creative outlet to release those painful feelings and thoughts. Remind yourself that you deserve better and define what deserving better means for you. And then, open your mind to believe it, open your heart to receive it, and watch how quickly you will achieve it. And so it is.

Journaling Exercise:

Draw a figure of yourself, and then a large bubble around it. Within that bubble write down all the beautiful vibrations that you hold. And then write down any negative vibrations that are weighing you down. Look at each negative word that is written in your bubble and visualize yourself releasing this energy from your body. Do this through your breath using deep exhalations. When you feel as though you have released this energetic vibration/memory/emotion/thought, cross the word out and move it to outside of the circle. Repeat this exercise until all the negativity has moved to the outside of your circle. And when you have finished, say out loud, "I command my sacred space." Next, write down the positive energy you wish to invite in. Bring these words into your circle. Feel the vibrations that the words hold and ask to receive them. You are creating the life that you desire. You are cocreating your destiny with the Universe.

Meditation:

Bring yourself into a deep meditative state by using your breath. Search within to find any stagnant energy in your aura. Do this by scanning your body and focus on looking for energy that feels stuck, blocked, or heavy. When you can identify this energy, use your breath to move it out of your energy field. Once released, invite in your manifested desire. Choose one of the positive words that you journaled about and envision the energy of that word. Feel that energy deeply. Imagine the energy of that word as a color, and envision that color pouring upon you from the sky above. Open your heart to receive this love. Repeat with as many of your chosen words as you wish.

I Speak My Boundaries with Confidence

Define: Creating, establishing, and communicating your boundaries are acts of self-love. Boundaries protect your energy, because their primary purpose is to ensure that you have a rewarding and fulfilling journey here on Earth. You are the star of your life; you are the leading character in this show, the main priority. But sometimes you forget this simple truth and sacrifice your own happiness in order to comfort another, in order to make their life perfect for them. There is so much goodness in your heart that you always want everyone else to be happy and living their truth, but while doing so, you forget about your own dreams and desires. But what about your life? What about your goals and happiness? Do you look after yourself entirely before channeling your energy into another? When we take care of ourselves first—mentally, physically, and spiritually—we, in turn, create an abundance of love and support to give others.

Boundaries are a set of rules and regulations that establishes the level of respect that you deserve. They outline ways to support your best interests so that you may feel grounded and in alignment with your soul at all times. If you find that you are feeling uneasy about certain situations or experiences, have a look and see if it is because your boundaries were crossed, or maybe you didn't communicate your boundaries properly, and so you feel depleted.

Today, create strong boundaries that best support your beliefs and dreams. Define the boundaries that protect your energy, and look after your mental health and well-being. Once you have established what those boundaries are, perfect them and communicate them with confidence. Know that with time they may change, so revisit them often. What you believe today may not be relevant to your belief system as you get older. Because as our awareness of ourselves and the world around us changes, so do our boundaries.

Speak your boundaries with ease, but be open to molding and changing them, just as your own energy molds and changes. Tune in to your own energy field and ensure that you are living your life according to these boundaries. And remember, the more love you give yourself, the more love you can share with everyone around you. This is how we will create love and peace in the world, by sharing the abundance of love and peace from within our hearts first.

Journaling Exercise:

If this affirmation has come up for you today, reflect over your life and pinpoint which memory is repeating itself in your head. Do you have a hard time letting it go because you didn't communicate your boundaries? In your journal, write down the incident. What happened, what you said or didn't say, and what the reaction was. Now accept that this happened. That this is the reality. And then, find a boundary that could have been spoken that would have protected your energy. Would you have been happier if you had said that boundary or acted according to that boundary? Visualize the person before you, the situation and scenario, and say that boundary out loud or do the action you desire. Repeat it in your head. Say "Thank you for the lesson" and then—let it go.

Meditation:

What boundary do you have the most difficulty expressing? Turn that boundary into a positive affirmation and into one sentence. For example, if your boundary was "I have difficulty saying no," turn that into "Saying no is an act of self-love." And repeat this affirmation in your head as you enter a deep state of relaxation. Continue to breathe with ease, as you sink deeper into the support of the Earth beneath you. Repeat the affirmation in your head intermittently as you choose to believe it to be true. Allow any feelings to arise within you, whether good or bad. Do not judge them. Let them simply be, and let them melt away. Use your affirmation to anchor your presence, and continue to breathe slowly as you enter deeper into your meditation.

I am safe, nurtured, and protected. I am calm. I am tranquil. I am living in a state of blissful peace. I am choosing this vibration by releasing any negative thoughts, pain, fear, or hurt into the ground, into the Earth. And I allow my energy to be renewed from the blessings above me. I am cleansed and rejuvenated. I am entering a state of tranquility by simply choosing to. And I relax. I release all that no longer serves me. I open myself to beauty, wonder, and enchantment. And I go about my day with ease, knowing that everything in my life is perfectly aligned.

I Have Everything That I Need in the Present Moment

Define: The present moment holds everything that you *need* right now. It holds pure peace and prosperity. It holds happiness, joy, and laughter. It does not hold pain, past regrets, anxious thoughts, or depressive feelings. It holds strength, courage, resilience, and love. The present moment is your answer to every question you could ever ask. The present moment is able to feed you all the love that you seek. It can heal your energy and raise your vibration up high. The present moment holds an invitation for transformation, for a new perception of your reality. And the moment you accept this invitation, your awareness of your life and everything in it will change. For you will be living with peace in your heart, and when you live in this space, you only want the best for everyone. Because when you are living in the present moment, you are truly aligned with your Higher Self, your soul, and the entire creation of the divine Universe. In the present moment there is an abundance of creativity from source energy. You can feel an unlimited amount of love around you and within you. In this beautiful safe space, you are one with the Universe.

But sometimes you allow your thoughts to carry you far away from this moment of truth. Sometimes you find yourself entertaining the ideas of others or chasing fickle vibrations. Sometimes you seek alternative pleasures that could be gained by accepting and living in the present moment. But you are choosing to make things more difficult than they need to be. Because although there will always be replicates of this pure energy around you, nothing will ever compare to what it feels like when you are living in alignment with the present moment. And to be with the present moment is so simple. It requires trust and patience as you focus on the world as it really is. Allow the world around you to dance before you as the miraculous, mysterious creation that it is. Use your breath to anchor stillness in your mind as you watch the events play out in your life with wonder and calm.

Today, allow your emotions and thoughts to float by as you make decisions from the voice of your soul. Live bravely and freely through the energy of your heart. Act according to your soul's desires, while feeding love and joyous vibrations to your mind and body. The more you practice living from this sacred space of pureness, the easier it will be to gravitate back into this heavenly moment as often as you like. The more we practice strengthening our spiritual tools, the stronger they become. And living in the present moment is one of the greatest gifts you can give yourself. It is always available; it is always ready and waiting for you. It is always going to welcome you. So, what are you waiting for? Hold your hands over your heart, take a deep breath, and tap into the energy of this deep peace that is residing within you.

Journaling Exercise:

On a scale of one to ten, how often do I live in the present moment?

What thoughts are occupying my time right now?

How can I release those thoughts?

How can I be more present in my daily activities?

How will the relationships change around me if I live more presently with myself and others?

Meditation:

Imagine the most beautiful place—real or fictional. And imagine yourself standing there, in this space. Take your time to define it. What makes it beautiful? The colors? The objects? The animals? The energy? This beautiful space that you have created is vibrating with the highest level of energetic love that you can imagine. Take your time to feel this energy and imagine its radiance. Sit or lie down in this sacred space as you allow the beautiful energy to fill your heart and soul until it overflows with positivity. Know that this is your safe space, your secret place of pureness. You can come back here any time that you wish.

I HAVE EVERYTHING THAT I NEED

You are and have always been enough. You are always growing, changing, and adapting and that's what makes you beautiful. Who you are today is not who you were yesterday, and it's not who you are going to be tomorrow. And each of those versions of yourself is enough. Because you are authentically living your truth. And by just simply being you is enough. You don't have to try and be more than what you already are, because you already are perfect. You are living the life you are meant to; everything in your life is right on time. You don't need to do a thing because you are and have always been enough.

I Am Divinely Guided by the Universe

Define: You are never alone in this world because you have a whole army of angelic energy beside you. They are helping you achieve your destiny by paving the pathway toward your greatest success. They are listening to the cravings of your soul; they are listening to all of the extraordinary things that you have ever wanted in the world. They have been with you for many lifetimes, guarding your safety from the galaxy above. They have been there through all of your triumphs and all of your misery. They help heal you. They help nurture you. They only ever want the best for you. They want you to fulfill your destiny. They want you to live your most incredible life filled with success, happiness, and love.

But sometimes when we speak our truth of what we want, we hold fear in our voice. Fear that we aren't worthy of receiving the miracles that we crave. Fear that we aren't worthy of receiving love, or that we aren't worthy of living the life that we have always desired. But this is all linked to the fear of absence. The fear that there is no great power looking over us or holding us lovingly. But deep down you know that this is untrue. You know that you are divinely supported by the Universe. But sometimes you forget.

If you have been feeling these false feelings lately, take a moment and look within. Feel the love within your heart, and listen to the voice of your soul sending you love. Your soul is telling you the pathway forward. Your soul is always connected to the angelic energy all around you, and you are being told to keep going. Call out to those angelic energies watching over you from the Universe. For they will tell you the truth. They will carry you forward and let you know that you are and have always been a divine creation of the Universe, destined to create incredible things. You are so loved. And your life is going to be filled with all the wondrous stories and experiences that you have always hoped for. Don't worry about a thing because your dreams are coming to you.

Today, speak your desires out loud and write the cravings of your soul amongst the stars. Trust and believe that you will receive these blessings because the whole Universe wants you to succeed. You are looked after by angels, ancestors, spirit guides, and angelic energy. They are all cheering you on and making sure you live the most incredible life here on Earth. So, talk to them. Tell them what you want, and listen to their guidance, as together you manifest your dreams into your reality.

Journaling Exercise:

What does my soul crave today?
What do I want to achieve in my life?
What messages do my angels and ancestors want to tell me?
What do I need to know today?

Meditation:

Close your eyes and envision your energetic presence in the Universe. See yourself as a golden figure of light, sitting amidst the cosmos above you. Feel the energy of your soul. Feel the incredible love that you hold within. Now ask to be shown the angelic energies around you. Allow their lights to glow brightly. These are your guides; these are your angels, your ancestors, and all the wonderful energies that are cheering you on. You are so loved. Allow yourself to feel this love. If you have questions for these angelic energies, take your time to connect with them, and ask them whatever questions you wish to know. Open your heart to receive their guidance. When you awake, write down any feelings or wisdom that have arisen from this experience.

I AM DIVINELY PROTECTED

PHOEBE GARNSWORTHY

I AFFIRM MY POWER

Moving through the different frequencies of life's challenges, I enter boldly. There is no fear, no space within me to move over to a vibration that is anything less than beautiful.

For it is love that breathes light within me and it is love that I feel around me.

I walk through life knowing that I have the power within me to heal myself.

I walk through life knowing that I have all the answers I need right now.

And I dance through my days with admiration for such a spectacular world of mystic, aligning with peace and patience for my life to unfold.

I do not rush, I do not worry, for I know that I'm divinely protected by the Universe at all times.

I Am in Alignment with My Higher Self

Define: Your Higher Self is your soul in the unseen realms. It is you, as the true energetic light being that you are. In this space, your soul is immersed in the great wisdom of source energy. This is where creation was birthed. Your Higher Self knows everything about your journey here. It knows the truth of your divinity, beauty, and talents. It knows the pathway of your life purpose and what you are destined to achieve in this life. Your Higher Self knows the answer to every question you could ever ask.

You are always connected to this pure version of yourself, but sometimes you forget. Sometimes you get caught up in low vibrations that hold you back from living your truth. Sometimes you get swept away in another's dream, thinking that you are finding your life purpose by helping them, by being with them, when really your life purpose is to be yourself.

So today, take a step closer to the real you. Break down any fears that are holding you back from aligning with your authentic self. Confront any limiting beliefs that are keeping you small and stopping you from being the courageous and beautifully talented divine being that you are.

You are brave, authentic, and full of loving light energy. It's time for you to embody the truth of your divine self. Reveal that version of yourself by making a choice to align with positive vibrations that illuminate your life. Allow any stagnant energy to simply melt away as you move with confidence closer to your Higher Self. Feel the way forward through the deep inner knowing of your intuition.

The more we consciously choose to surround ourselves with vibrations that illuminate our life, the closer we come to embodying the divine truth of who we really are. Let go of any scenarios, people, or places that are holding you back from shining brightly. Choose to surround yourself with like-minded individuals who celebrate the truth of what it means to be themselves. Applaud your individuality, your uniqueness, your authenticity. And keep releasing, keep breathing, keep aligning with who it is that you really are.

"I am in alignment with my Higher Self.
I feel at peace and as one with the Universe.
I am loved, protected, and cared for.
My Higher Self is always looking after me,
making sure I receive the right lessons along my journey
to bring forth the greatest experience for my life."

Journaling Exercise:

What activities light up my soul?
How often do I participate in these activities?
How can I do them more often?
What environments bring me peace and joy?
How often do I visit these places?
When can I visit my favorite place next?

Meditation:

Envision what your Higher Self looks like. There is no right or wrong concept; just allow your imagination to take charge. Your Higher Self may change with time, so simply imagine the most beautiful, pure version of yourself that you can. Once you see your Higher Self, walk toward it slowly, saying the affirmation in your head: "I am in alignment with my Higher Self." As you reach your Higher Self, step into that pure version of you, and completely embody it. Feel the vibrations that it exudes. Feel the energy you possess as you mold into your true self. Continue to breathe steadily as you truly embody the energy of your Higher Self. Let go and release any hesitation that you may feel. Align deeper into your Higher Self with every breath. Stay in this space for as long as possible. When you feel aligned with it, ask your Higher Self any questions or guidance that you need to know. Trust that the answers you receive are what you need to know today.

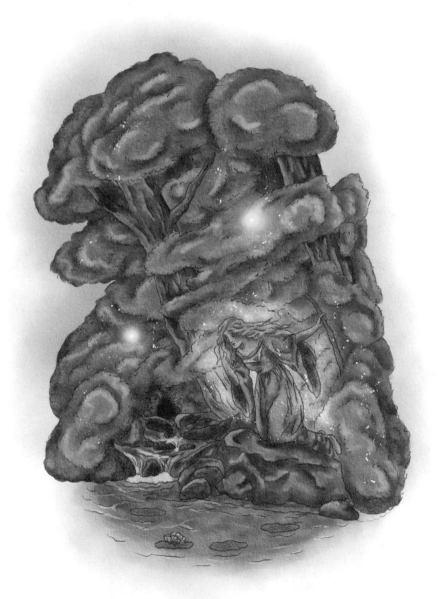

I am in love with the divine within me.
I am gracing the shores of endless talents and my gifts are flowing in abundance.
My life purpose is clear and effortless,
for I have always been working toward this goal unconsciously.
Yet nothing is by chance, my soul always knew.
And as I take a step back and fall down,
I am simply reminded to trust in myself once more.
I have the power to be whoever I desire.
I have the ability to mold and change my life as I choose.
I am in alignment with my Higher Self,
and from this place anything is possible.

I Accept the Present Moment and Let Go of Expectations

Define: At every moment of every day, trust and believe that all of your needs are being wonderfully met at all times. Let go of expectations, of the desire to control your life, and accept yourself right here in the present moment. If we hold on tightly to preconceived ideas about how we think our life should be, we lose sight of the gift that is being presented to us right now. If we focus our attention on what we want or need, we forget that we are, in this very moment, more than enough. The pathway to inner peace and complete gratitude for your life starts by living wholeheartedly in the present moment. Any vibration that you crave of peace, love, or happiness can be discovered right here, right now, in the present moment. In order for you to gain such a powerful insight into the miracles that surround you and that are manifesting for you, you must first believe that you are living them right now.

If you find yourself immersed in despair, with no clear opening for a way out—or if you feel desperate for your life to change but can't figure out the way forward—find peace in the unknowing. Hold faith that things will change when the time is right. But in order for life to change, you need to honor and accept yourself in this very moment. If you continue to suppress your current life obstacles, they will only grow until you move through them. The present moment holds your invitation for change. The present moment holds the ability to open your mind and heart to see the truth of what blissful miracles lie within you and around you. All you need to do is embrace these gifts by letting go of any expectations you place upon yourself.

The present moment holds no space for fear or pain. The present moment is completely neutral, calm, and worry-free. The more comfortable you become in your own silence, cleansing your mind of your struggles or painful thoughts, the easier it will be for you to receive the gift that is available to you. In the present moment you can find every answer to what you are searching for. Here you can connect with the spirit world and receive the wisdom from your soul and all the angelic entities that surround you. Through silence, their love travels faster. And in the present moment, this love is always laid out before you to take. Open your heart to receive these blessings. Take a deep breath in and out as you surrender your desires into the present moment. Trust and believe that all is as it should be. Ground your soul into your body as you align with your Higher Self and allow your energy to rise up and rejoice with the miraculous creations of the Universe's love that surround you.

Journaling Exercise:

What is stopping me from living in the present moment right now?
What expectations do I place upon myself and my life?
What kind of life do I crave?
What do I need to let go of to live more fully in my own energy?
What do I need to accept in my life?
How can I do this?

Meditation:

Bring your awareness to the space between your eyebrows at the center of your forehead, in your third-eye energy chakra. Imagine this focal point as a magnet to your energy. Call all of your energy that has expanded outside of you back into this space just behind your eyes. Imagine all of your energy outside of your body and feel it magnetize back into this space. Breathe slowly and deeply as you continue to draw all of your energy back to your third-eye chakra. As the energy continues to fill this space, allow it to fall down along your spine and into your pelvis. Feel your body become very heavy, as you regain your energy from outside of you and transform this energy into greatness. Let this energy pour into the center of the Earth. Imagine the energy from Mother Earth moving around your body and gifting yourself love. Sit here for as long as you like.

I Have Clarity over My Day—
My Mind Is Clear and Worry-Free

Define: You know the truth of what is really going on in your life right now. You know the answers to every question circulating in your mind. How? Because your soul has been speaking the solutions to you. Your spirit guides have been trying to send you messages and signs to confirm the truth you already know. But sometimes your mind thinks too loudly, and it drowns the voice of your intuition. Sometimes there are outside distractions holding you back from seeing the truth that resides in your heart. And so, the feeling of confusion over what is right and wrong can feel overwhelming. It's okay, though. Do not suffocate inside your stress. Take a deep breath and let the answers present themselves to you. All you need to do is take a moment to yourself to honor your soul, clear your mind, and ground your energy.

The more time you spend immersed in the love of your own vibration, the clearer your mind will become. There is no space in your divine self for false vibrations. Low vibrations do not live in the high frequencies that you can create so easily in your life. When we focus our attention on the spiritual practices that provide self-love and self-care, we are able to harmonize the flow of energy between our mind, body, and soul. This will bring forth the great clarity that you seek, as your perception of the world becomes completely transparent. You don't need to hold on to these worries in your life, because source energy is protecting you from living them. You don't need to stress about what's happening or not happening in your life, because your soul is going to guide you through to where it is that you need to be. Have faith and trust that your world is exactly as it needs to be right now, and that you have the power to make the changes that you seek if you so wish.

Remind yourself of the strength of your own inner knowing. Trust in its power to lead you along your pathway. If you feel worried or weak, listen to the voice of your soul, and let it remind you that you will never be led astray.

You will never be taken to a place where you cannot overcome your challenges. Every element on your life path, as difficult as it may be, is predestined for you. It's there for you to move through it and succeed past it, so that your soul can transform into greatness. With every obstacle that you triumph over, wisdom will be delivered to you.

You are always divinely guided by the Universe, your spirit guides, and your Higher Self. You are always immersed in an abundance of love and light to support and hold you. Do not fear the confusion, for the truth will always prevail. And the truth is, you are always supported and guided to live the greatest life that you desire. Let the voice of your intuition lead the way forward. Remind yourself of the strength within to be your own warrior of light as you persevere through these times of darkness.

Journaling Exercise:

Do I have clarity over my life path? Why? Why not?
What is my soul trying to tell me today?
How can I enable strength in my mental health?
What spiritual practices provide me with the greatest peace?
How can I incorporate those spiritual practices into my life more?

Meditation:

At the beginning of your meditation, imagine yourself sitting on top of a mountain where there is an abundance of air blowing gently on your skin. Call upon the energy of Air to soothe your emotions and bring forth clarity to your mind. Slowly breathe in the air around you and envision it cleansing all the energy inside your mind and body. As you blow your breath back out, release any tension that is holding you back from seeing the truth of who you are and where you are going. Any fears, pain, lies, or trauma—let it go with each breath. With every breath in, invite in clarity, prosperity, and peace. Repeat this breathing exercise until you feel your energy align with the soothing vibrations of the Universe.

My Angels Are Always with Me, Keeping Me Safe and Protected

Define: There is nothing to fear, for you are divinely protected and guided by your angels at all times. There is nothing to worry about, for you are walking the exact life path that you were always meant to walk. These beautiful angelic energies that surround you are majestic spirits, or ancestors who have passed over. They are your spirit guides. They are working together to support your growth in this life. They are conversing with the Universe on your behalf, making sure you are receiving all of the powerful life lessons, all of the wisdom and confidence that you have been seeking. And they are sending you love, so much love, from afar. Letting you know that they are always with you.

Your angels are here to tell you a message today. They are here to let you know that now is the time for you to follow your passions and dreams. They want you to know that they have been sending you messages, and the messages that you thought might be from them . . . were true! They want to remind you to always look at your lifestyle to reveal what is making your vibrations low, and to make the changes in your life that support your ultimate goals. They are telling you that you will be safe and protected when you put yourself first, and that this is the true pathway forward.

Your angels are always sending you messages in the real world. These messages can come in the form of words through strangers, through peculiar synchronicities, or through animals and birds. Whatever you find your attention drawn to, recognize the power in the message that is awaiting. Let your first thought guide you. Let your intuition speak loudly.

Your angels are speaking through your intuition too. Although our intuition is the voice of our soul, our soul is always immersed in the angelic realm. In this place of pureness and safety, your soul receives messages from your angels to give to you too. You are forever connected to this beautiful divine light that surrounds you, always. Ask anything that you need to know, and you will be guided to the answer. But sometimes, it is difficult to trust that voice, because perhaps it has been a while since your last conversation. But it's never too late to ignite that connection again. Talk to your soul often. Talk to your spirit guides, talk to your angels, talk to the divine entities who guard and protect you from the angelic realm. They only want the best for you. They will never leave you. You are always safe with them by your side.

Journaling Exercise:

Who are my angels?
What energy are they gifting me today?
What are my angels saying to me today?
What problems do I need guidance with today?
What advice do my angels want me to hear?

Meditation:

Your intention is to meet your angels. In a meditative state, imagine a beautiful golden stairwell in front of you. Spend your time defining this stairwell, and as you walk up it, say your intention out loud in your mind several times. Continue to breathe slowly and steadily. Take your time. As you finally reach the top of the stairwell, stand and wait there for your angel(s) to come to you. They might be there already waiting for you. Or this practice may take repetition. Allow whatever image that comes into your vision to be so. If you cannot see anything, feel the energy that is being gifted. Trust and believe. Spend as long as you wish speaking with your angel(s) and ask for the guidance you need to know today.

MY ANGELS ARE WITH ME

I see you clearly.

I feel your energy.

I know your face.

There is something so familiar about your presence,

yet I have never met you before.

Or have I?

Have you been with me for many lifetimes?

Have we chosen to look after one another in these worlds?

Do we care for each other, guide each other, and send each other love?

Because I feel you with me always.

I feel safe, nurtured, and protected from your love.

I hear your messages, I see the signs.

I know that you are healing me.

I know that you are guiding me towards my greatest achievement.

I know that I am never alone.

I know that I am divinely supported and guided by your love at all times,

and for that, I thank you.

I Always Have Everything That I Need

Define: You have everything that you need right here in your heart. You are surrounded with an abundance of love from the Universe, and this love vibrates for an eternity. It is always supporting you and guiding you along your life path. You have the power to heal yourself, to gift yourself love and peace, from the natural vibrations of the Universal energies that surround you. Mother Nature is at your doorstep, gifting you nurturing, healing energy through her love. She supports your mission to succeed on this Earth and provides you with the platform to ground your soul into your body so that you may walk confidently toward your life mission. You are surrounded with fresh air to breathe, providing you with clarity in your mind so that you may understand the world around you with ease. And you have the sun, a blazing fire of stardust, who feeds you health and vibrant light, enabling you to thrive in this world through his unconditional love. You have fresh water to drink, to quench your thirst and soothe your emotions, providing you with great peace in your heart. There are many blessings around you; all you need to do is open your eyes to see them.

Gratitude attracts more gratitude. And the more we choose to see all of the wonderful things in our life to be grateful for, the more blessings will come our way. It's perfectly okay to want things that you don't have, and although it can be frustrating to wait, wondering if they will ever come to you, hold faith that they will. Because if what you desire is what your soul truly craves, then you will always receive it. It may come to you a little later than expected, or looking different than anticipated, but it will come to you and bring you all the happiness, peace, and joy that you've been dreaming about and so much more.

You don't need to stress or worry that what you have is not enough, because your very existence shows that this is not true. Your soul, your spirit guides, and your angels have all ensured that your life is filled with all the blessings that you could possibly need right here at this moment. But if you crave something different from what you hold, listen to your soul and check in to see whether this is truly needed. And then, leap forward toward this new goal, trusting and believing that the Universe will catch you, raise you high, and deliver you everything that you need and so much more.

"I have everything that I need right here at this moment.
I am always surrounded with love from the Universe.
I am always supported and protected by my angels.
I am always guided by my Higher Self.
I am and have always been enough."

Journaling Exercise:
What am I grateful for today?
What do I have in my life right now that, once upon a time, I wished for?
What do I need in my life?
The things that I need, are they what my soul truly craves?
What can I do to call in these desires?
What am I doing in my life that welcomes in these needs?

Meditation:
Choose one of your greatest desires, and let's manifest it in this meditation. Use your breath to enter a deep meditation and then envision that desire coming true in your life. Imagine yourself living with that goal; imagine that this is your reality. Feel the energy that this goal brings into your life. Feel the high frequencies that support you as they raise your vibration up to reach this goal. Sit with this energy for a while, letting it completely consume you. Allow yourself to align with this desire. Speak your manifestation to the Universe, and then trust and believe that it will be delivered in the divine time. And then—let it go. Have faith that all is as it should be.

I Am Always Learning How to Be Better

Define: Your perception of the world around you is based on your experience in this life and the wisdom that you have acquired over your past lives. We are also influenced by ancestral trauma as well as the actions of others, and we create an understanding of our life based on all of these factors. Throughout our life, this perception is going to change because we are going to change. We are going to endure new life lessons, new challenging experiences, and these will ultimately transform our understanding of the world for the better. But in order for our perception to evolve wisely, with our best interests at heart, we need to be flexible to change and open to accepting that our beliefs may be outdated.

At some point in our life, we may be faced with a conflict that forces us to face the fact that our beliefs are wrong and that we need to change them. It could be the result of our own experience, inherited beliefs, or having been given wrong information from someone we trusted and admired. Often, in our childhood, we adopt beliefs that may be corrupted or influenced in an unhealthy way, in order for our survival. And to change these beliefs could feel uncomfortable or heartbreaking, for we are forced to humble ourselves to learn how to be better. But learning how to be better is an important key in our personal development journey. To be flexible to change and to open ourselves up to failure are strong qualities to hold, for they will enable profound growth to be gifted to us when the time is right.

Our wisdom is gained through our healing, through our personal development of triumphing over trauma and pain. We will never know all the wisdom that is needed, for we are always evolving. We are constantly transforming and facing new challenges, new invitations, and new opportunities for growth. And we can discover as much wisdom as possible when we are open to curiosity.

Today, release everything that you think you know and be open to receiving new information, new vibrations on how to be better. Our life is a playground of learning and unlearning. And today, whatever has happened is asking you to unlearn something in your mind. Fall down humbly so that you may rise again with strength. For as you rise you will lift others up around you. Focus your new understanding with love at the center of your belief system, and see the divine truth of wholeness achieved as you attune your flow of energy in harmony with others. You have the power to truly make a difference in this world and to create a life that you are proud of, proud to leave for those who come after you. Use your voice and action to create the changes that build a prosperous future for all. To ignite new beginnings, we need to open our mind in ways it has never opened before. This is done by unlearning and relearning, and being humble as we learn from one another. You have great transformation at your fingertips; choose to open the door before you and listen to the wisdom within you.

Journaling Exercise:

What belief do I hold that could be the result of another influence?
What do I believe about myself or another that is not true?
How can I change that belief system?
Who could I talk to or what advice could I use to change that belief?
How can I feed love into that belief to look at my life differently and create
    more peace?

Meditation:

In a state of meditation, imagine the entire world as though you are viewing it from the galaxy. See the beauty of the Earth spinning around and envision small, glowing lights representing all the people who are living on the Earth. Allow that light to rise up from the Earth, and tune in to its energetic frequency. Can you feel the love and peace that it provides? Focus on being a harmonious addition to that beauty. See the energy as a color of light and imagine yourself giving and receiving this loving light energy. See this energy swirl around the Earth. Allow yourself to be completely immersed in its beauty.

Miracles Are Coming to Me

Define: Miracles are coming to you. Why? Because you are worthy of receiving them. You are a divine creation of the Universe's love, and because of this, you will be gifted with all of the glorious experiences and majestic rewards that you desire. The only request of the Universe is that you live your life authentically as yourself in order to receive your blessings. When we live authentically in alignment with our true self, we walk our life path with complete confidence and ease, for we can hear the voice of our intuition loudly. Here in this space we are open to receiving guidance toward our blessings in the most unusual of ways. When we are content and at peace with who we are, we have faith in our future. We know that the Universe will never deliver us something that we cannot overcome, nor will we ever receive something that isn't in our best interest. We know this truth because we have unshakable faith in the Universe, faith in our soul's path, and faith in our soul contract. Because of these beliefs, our life will always be blessed with miracles. If something is laying in your pathway that you perceive to be difficult or a deterrent from what you desire, look deeper into the meaning as to how you can use it to your advantage to obtain your dreams and wishes. Can you grow stronger through the transformation process of letting go and changing direction? Dive deep within it to see how you can find the positive and apply that positivity to your life.

Your greatest pathway is laid out before you. Your destiny was written before you entered this life. Your life journey is full of both triumphs and failures, and they will equally bring you profound depths of emotion, and wisdom. The more confidently you walk along your pathway, willing to flow with the natural vibrations of the Universe's love, the more easily the miracles that you desire will come forth to you. It is merely a matter of believing in your own power, knowing that the whole Universe is supporting you, sending you love, and delivering you the miracles that you have asked for.

Speak your dreams and aspirations clearly to the Universe and allow the entire cosmic creation to deliver what you have asked for. Angelic entities, your ancestors, and spirit guides are all watching you from above. They are sending you signs and showing you how to move forward. But it's up to you to be open to receiving those messages. Talk to the Universe often and listen for the signs, because miracles are waiting to arrive, and your manifestations are ready to come into fruition.

Journaling Exercise:

Am I living authentically in alignment with myself?
What miracles do I want today?
How do I know that the Universe is supporting me?
What could a sign be in my life from my spirit guides and angelic entities?
Are there any obstacles in my life that I need to learn how to flow with?
How can I turn my difficulties into a positive lesson?

Meditation:

In a deep state of meditation, move your awareness to the top of your head. Focus on the energy here. See the energy swirling in a fluid circle of angelic stardust. It is resembling a crown. Allow that circle of energy to continuously flow around with ease. As you focus your attention on this space, allow the crown of angelic stardust to continue to expand upward and outward. It is turning into a funnel, and you now have the power to invite in all the blessings, love, and cosmic creations from the Universe above. Whatever you desire, ask for it. Ask for your manifestations. Ask how you can cocreate these wishes with the power of your spirit guides. Take your time conversing with Spirit in this space. Allow your energy to radiate and uplift as you connect back to where you come from, into the cosmic energy of source creation.

Today I choose peace.

I choose to feel the harmonious vibrations that echo within my soul.

I choose to seek refuge in the peaceful energy that soothes my being.

At any point I know I can relax my mind by breathing this gentle energy that flows within me and around me.

And if I somehow forget this truth, I simply close my eyes, take a deep breath, and bring myself back home.

I Welcome Change into My Life, Knowing That It Is Always for My Greater Good

Define: Every element of your life is pushing you forward to become the person you have always dreamed of. There is no other option than for you to step into this version of yourself that you have been craving. But in order to get there, you need to be open to change, even if it seems impossible. Sometimes we have an idea of the type of life path that we need to live in order to be that person. And we hold expectations upon ourselves and then find ourselves in pain when our life doesn't pan out the way we thought it would. But when we do this, we are dismissing the truth that our Higher Self and the Universe always know the best route to get us where we want to be. You are destined to step into greatness. It is written into your soul contract for you to evolve and rejoice with great rewards and profound wisdom. Your life experience is destined to include great depths of emotions and incredible growth. So even if the change that is laid out before you appears to be disappointing or painful, lean into it curiously and be open to the possibility that it could be everything that you have ever wanted and more.

Today, let go of any expectations of how you think your life should unfold, and trust and believe that it is exactly the way it is meant to be. Stop looking at that closed door and take a step forward on the pathway that is open before you. This pathway is going to lead you toward your greatest success and your greatest adventure. It may feel uncomfortable, or not be what you hoped for, but trust that you are moving forward into the ultimate life you have always wished you were living. You are about to embark upon the most incredible journey that you could ever imagine. But to get there, you need to trust the process. You need to listen to your intuition. Be open to the signs. Build unbreakable faith and confidence with the Universe. Believe that you are divinely guided and loved wholeheartedly by the angelic energy that is all around you. Because you always are. Whenever a door is closing before you, it is closing for you. It is closing because there is nothing there for you anymore. There is nothing there that will support your evolution of greatness in this world. So, be brave as you trust in the mystery of new beginnings. See this change as a positive light before you and let go of the negative connotations that you may feel attached with. Today, open your heart to receive this love as you step into your true power. Lean curiously into this change that is presented before you. The only person who is holding you back is yourself. The time is now.

Journaling Exercise:

What change am I resisting in my life right now?
What could be a positive outcome of this change?
How can I focus my attention to welcome this change?
What expectations have I preconceived about my life?
What can I do to let go of those expectations?

Meditation:

In a deep state of meditation, imagine you are climbing a hill. With each step forward, feel the strength of the Universe beneath your feet, encouraging you to keep walking. With each step, use your breath to release any expectations, limiting beliefs, or past heartache. Keep moving forward. Take your time climbing this hill. When you are ready, allow yourself to reach the top of the hill and sit down. See what a miraculous climb you have endured and the sweet reward that now awaits you. Explore the incredible view of the horizon that you have achieved by your persistence. You can see everything so clearly now. You understand the reasons why, and you are thankful for the difficult climb to get here. Sit here for a while and allow the energy of Air to bring forth clarity and peace into your mind. If you feel called to, ask for guidance from your spirit guides who surround you. They will tell you anything that you wish to know.

I Welcome Love into My Life with an Open Heart

Define: There is so much love surrounding you. You are connected to the entire cosmic Universe full of high vibrations and loving energy at all times. You are woven into this cosmic web, and therefore, all of this love that vibrates around you is vibrating within you. You are surrounded with love from angelic beings, from star-seed energy, from archangels and spirit guides, from ancestors and Mother Nature's creations. And every single one of them is sending you love and health throughout your journey, every step of the way. You are not only surrounded with love from your angelic guides in the unseen realms but also here on Earth, through relationships, friendships, and family. But far too often, you don't believe you are worthy of receiving this love. Sometimes you like to believe that you are all alone on this journey. But that is simply not true because you always have the most incredibly profound love around you; you just need to start believing in it.

Feel the love that surrounds you. Feel the love that already resides within you. Get comfortable in giving and receiving love to and from yourself through the spirit world, so that when someone comes into your life to show you that they want to love you, you can show them how. Because you will have filled yourself up with so much love from the cosmic intelligence that to share that love with another will be a natural extension. Learning how to love each other takes patience and time, but it starts with open communication, listening to our intuition, and speaking our boundaries. When these three things are aligned, the love that you receive will be a sweet addition to the already fruitful life that you have created for yourself.

So today, listen clearly—you are worthy of receiving all of the greatest love you could ever possibly imagine! But know that when this love enters your life, it will actually be more powerful and more beautiful than what you imagined to be possible. Because it is a love that has evolved and expanded across many lifetimes. It is a love that overflows with an abundance of miraculous vibrations that you deserve. Because you do deserve this kind of love. Love will come to you in many forms—through relationships, friendships, family, animals, and angelic spirits. There are so many opportunities for love to be delivered to you, but in order to receive this love you need to open your heart to believe in it. You need to have confidence and faith that you are worthy of receiving it. Tune in to the frequencies within and around you and allow that love to blossom. Continue to gift yourself self-love and self-care as you harness these high vibrations. And when you finally embody the truth of your divine self, your heart will naturally open to believe you are worthy of receiving the greatest love possible.

Journaling Exercise:

What is holding me back from believing I am worthy of receiving love?
How can I move through my fears to be open to receiving this love?
What can I do in my daily life to embody self-love and self-care?
What activities am I already doing that support my own self-love?
How can I be kinder to myself?

Meditation:

Close your eyes and imagine a golden-colored gate in front of you. Spend some time defining the gate. Feel the energy of this golden glow illuminating in front of you. The gate represents your willingness to let love in. Imagine the gate as though it is the opening of your heart, and slowly, with each breath, allow that gate to open completely. The gate may open quickly, or it may be a little bit stuck. Use your breath to enable a steady opening of the gate, so that once it is open, it will stay open. If you find it difficult to open the gate, allow any feelings or fears that are holding you back to come to the surface, face them, enter them, and then let them go. Take your time to open the gate and let love in.

I Am Calm; I Choose My Thoughts

Define: Your thoughts do not define you. Say it with me: "My thoughts do not define me." Your thoughts are separate from who you really are. They do not influence or decipher the true beauty of your soul. Your thoughts are simply a product of your brain, whose purpose is to solve problems. The thought that you hold on to is only there because it's asking for a solution. It actually wants to be let go of. But your brain keeps throwing ideas at you, ideas that don't serve a purpose to support or love you. Those ideas merely provide a logical explanation or exploration of that thought. Your brain isn't choosing to give you positive or negative support; it is simply providing suggestions and solutions, which is what the brain does. But you—you have the power to choose which idea or thought you want to listen to, and then from there your brain will unravel and continue to suggest proof or ideas as to why that thought was true. So choose the thoughts that honor your soul and provide you with the opportunity to align with your greatest self. It's you who decides the future of your thoughts. You get to decide whether you should listen to them or let them go. You have that power over your brain and over your thoughts. Because your soul is the true leader over your mind. Your soul is able to navigate your life path with loving vibrations, so let your soul speak clearly. Trust the voice of your intuition as you choose which thoughts are important for you to keep.

If you find yourself holding tightly to a thought that doesn't serve your best interest, simply let that thought go. And replace that empty space with a new thought. Choose a thought that inspires you. Choose a thought that uplifts you. Choose a thought that feeds love to you. Any ideas or beliefs that are holding you back from being you, from being true to yourself, or from succeeding in life, let those thoughts go. You have the power to live the life that you desire. And you will live that life by choosing thoughts that align with your Higher Self. By choosing actions and beliefs that encourage love to blossom from within you and around you. Choose the thoughts that support your greatest good and that enable you to stride with confidence and happiness toward your goal and dreams.

So today, if you are holding on to any thoughts, fears, or beliefs that are stopping you from being your greatest self, then let those thoughts go. Simply use your breath to release the attachment of any thought that you are fixated on. Spend as long as you need releasing whatever has been hindering your growth. Confront your thoughts with loving intentions, yet question their authenticity. When you finally realize that it is serving you no more, let it go. Invite a new thought in that brings you peace and support. Choose thoughts that encourage the beautiful, intelligent version of yourself that you really are. It's time to take back your power.

Journaling Exercise:

What thoughts are no longer serving me?
What limiting beliefs can I let go of today?
What are some positive thoughts that I can choose to focus on?
What thoughts enable me to be my greatest self?
What's a positive affirmation of something I am aspiring to step into?

Meditation:

Close your eyes and bring your awareness to your breath as you breathe in and out slowly. As you focus on your breath, allow yourself to sink deeper into relaxation, allowing the Earth beneath you to support you. Let yourself be nurtured and loved by the Universe in this sacred space. Melt into the loving vibrations of Mother Nature and allow your mind to empty out completely. Any thoughts that arise, let them arise, but do not linger upon their existence. You choose to let those thoughts go, and you do so easily. Continue to breathe and focus on feeling the love and support that surrounds you. Pick one of your favorite ideas that support your greater good and choose to focus on it. Embody the energy of what that belief means to you and allow your soul to absorb that feeling entirely. Continue to breathe slowly as you rewrite your vibration to reflect your ultimate desires.

Today Is a New Day

I open my eyes and focus my attention on the present moment. Today is a new day. Everything that has happened before me has melted into the memories of yesterday. I feel no stress in my body, no fear or pain as I focus on the present moment. I enter deep breaths as I welcome this beautiful, perfect new day. I am at peace with my past. I am open to the discoveries of what may come to me in the future, but I do not look so far forward that I forget the incredible magic of what today can bring. I am confident in my choices. I am happy in my surroundings. I am calm, relaxed, and full of loving energy. I listen to the cravings of my soul and move my vibration to the sounds of its yearnings. And from here, I focus my energy on nurturing that passion, allowing deep, loving vibrations to move through my essence, filling me up with joy, with happiness, and with pure bliss! Today is a new day.

Love, Phoebe

About the Author

Phoebe Garnsworthy writes books that speak to your soul.
She is an Australian female author who seeks to discover magic in everyday
life. She travels between the worlds of the seen and unseen, gathering ancient
wisdom and angelic energy. Her writings reflect a dance with the mystical and
wonderful, an intoxicating love potion to devour in a world that overflows
with forgotten love and enchantment. The intention of her writing is to
encourage conscious living and unconditional love.

www.PhoebeGarnsworthy.com

Other Books by Phoebe Garnsworthy

Daily Rituals: Positive Affirmations to Attract Love, Happiness and Peace

Would you like to attract more abundance? More love, more happiness, and more peace? It is available to you right now, if you believe it to be true. Everything in existence is vibrating energy. Whatever you want can be yours—if you learn how to emit that vibrational frequency. And from this place, energy will magnetize toward you, naturally connecting like vibrations together. This enables you to attract what it is you wish to seek.

Align with Soul: A Spiritual Guide to Transform Your Life

In every challenge, we are handed an opportunity to evolve into a better version of ourselves. We can learn how to heal and navigate a fulfilling life path by aligning with our soul to activate the wisdom of the Universal love that surrounds us. *Align with Soul* provides you with the spiritual philosophy, tools, and techniques to inspire your journey of personal development toward enlightenment.

Remember the Witch Within: Magical Studies of Our Past Lives

We all share a history of witches. Our great ancestors were the first to weave the wisdom of the spirit realm, but they were stopped from passing this knowledge on to us. In this book, Phoebe reveals the truth of their divinity as she explores her past lives and the lives of her ancestors in a hypnosis state of past-life regression. Seven chapters, seven lives, seven stories that remind us of the feminine power that has been suppressed but has not been forgotten. Let us remember the witch within.

Sacred Space Rituals: A Spiritual Guide to Nurture Your Inner Power

This book was created by calling upon ancient spiritual philosophies from around the world. It primarily uses the principles of creative visualization while harnessing the abundance of Universal energies that surround you. The purpose of these rituals is to assist you in your journey of personal development and spiritual transformation.

Define Me Divine Me: A Poetic Display of Affection

This poetry book is an exploration of raw truth that provokes our deepest emotions so that we may honor both the light and the dark within us. Together, we allow the words of enlightened wisdom and painful beginnings to wash through us as we stand back up and claim what is rightfully ours.

and still, the Lotus Flower Blooms: A Spiritual Soul's Pathway to Self-Confidence

This poetry book explores the hardships we face throughout our life and inspires you to search within to find the tools you need to survive. Like the lotus flower who grows through mud yet rises every day to greet the sunshine without a slither of darkness upon its petals, you, too, will move through your life with grace, resilience, and beauty.

Lost Nowhere and Lost Now Here: A Journey of Self-Discovery in a Magical World

The *Lost Nowhere* and *Lost Now Here* book series explores spiritual witchcraft in a fictional environment. While following the eclectic imagination of a girl called Lily, the reader is taken to another universe, to a magical world called Sa Neo. In this enchanted world, you will meet powerful witches, shamans, healers, queens, kings, and mermaids. You will heed their spiritual wisdom, while having all of your senses heightened, as you explore a world of beauty, magic, and miracles.